A BIBLIOGRAPHY

OF

HENRY DAVID THOREAU

A BIBLIOGRAPHY OF

HENRY DAVID THOREAU

COMPILED BY FRANCIS H. ALLEN

BOSTON AND NEW YORK

HOUGHTON MIFFLIN COMPANY

MDCCCCVIII

JOHNSON REPRINT CORPORATION   JOHNSON REPRINT COMPANY LIMITED
111 Fifth Avenue, New York, N.Y. 10003 Berkeley Square House, London, W. 1

PS
3052
.A44
1967

First reprinting, 1967, Johnson Reprint Corporation

Printed in the United States of America

PREFACE

THE general plan of this book is based on the bibliographies which have preceded it in the series, but certain departures have been made, in accordance with what appeared to be the particular demands of the matter to be presented. The division-headings are, however, self-explanatory, so that it seems unnecessary to say anything further here as to the contents and arrangement, and we may proceed at once to the acknowledgments which, in common with all other bibliographers, the compiler of this book owes to the many persons who have helped him in his labors.

To his predecessors in the field of Thoreau bibliography, first of all, the compiler owes a great debt, especially to Dr. Samuel Arthur Jones, whose admirable "Bibliography of Henry David Thoreau," published by the Rowfant Club of Cleveland in 1894, virtually complete as far as it goes in all the most important particulars, the present writer at the beginning of his work made a sort of base of operations for his own campaign. Further assistance of the same kind was also obtained from the bibliography by Mr. John P. Anderson of the British Museum, appended to Mr. Salt's Life of Thoreau.

The books and periodicals examined were mainly found in the great public and semi-public libraries of Boston, New York, and Cambridge. A large part of the work was done at the Boston Public Library and the Boston Athenæum, frequent visits were made to the Harvard University Library and the Massachusetts State Library, and many hours were spent in the Public Library at Concord, Massachusetts, and in the Lenox and Astor Libraries and the Columbia University Library in New York, to all of which institutions the compiler is grateful, not only for the usual privileges of readers, but in many cases for special kindnesses and attentions. In particular he desires to thank Mr. William C. Lane of the Harvard Library and Miss Kelley of Concord for favors extended to him. To three private collections also the compiler is under heavy obligations. Mr. Stephen H. Wakeman of New York, whose collection of first editions of Thoreau is a particularly interesting and valuable one, and who is now the fortunate possessor of Thoreau's original manuscript journals, has been very kind and helpful. To Mrs. J. Chester Chamberlain of New York the compiler is grateful for the privilege of examining the Thoreau material contained in the collection of the late Mr. Chamberlain. Mr. Herbert W. Hosmer of Concord, Massachusetts, the present owner of the Thoreau collection made by his late brother, Mr. Alfred W. Hosmer, has very hospitably permitted the compiler to spend many hours with his collection, which is especially rich in biographical and critical matter concerning Thoreau, — a department which is ignored by

most collectors. Grateful thanks must also be
extended to the Misses Hosmer of Concord for
many kindnesses, and to Mr. Edwin B. Hill of
Lakeland, Michigan, Colonel Thomas Wentworth
Higginson, Mr. Charles E. Goodspeed, and the
Rev. George Willis Cooke for assistance in various
ways. Mr. Luther S. Livingston, besides permit-
ting the use of the Thoreau matter printed in his
"American Book-Prices Current," has been kind
enough to supply the record of this year's sales in
advance of the publication of his 1908 volume,
and in other ways has been helpful.

The compiler is especially grateful to three
gentlemen who have had the kindness to read
his proofs and make valuable suggestions, — Dr.
Samuel A. Jones, the author of the earlier bibliography before mentioned, whose hearty coöper-
ation has been a source of great satisfaction to
the compiler and whose friendly letters have been
a spur to his spirits; Mr. Patrick Kevin Foley of
Boston, known to all American book-collectors,
whose keen but genial criticism has been especially
helpful; and Mr. F. B. Sanborn, who has not
spared of his intimate and extensive knowledge
of Thoreau and his works in assisting the compiler
to make this book as complete and accurate as
possible. Finally, the compiler owes a debt of
gratitude to Mr. George B. Ives, not only for
special assistance in various ways, but most of all
for the many valuable suggestions obtained from
a study of his excellent Bibliography of Oliver
Wendell Holmes, which has been at once the ad-

miration and the despair of at least one of his
successors in this bibliographical series. Thoreau's
magazine contributions and other fugitive pieces
were so few, however, and Mr. Sanborn and
others have been so diligent in searching them
out, that it was not to be expected that any such
interesting discoveries could be made in that department of Thoreau bibliography as were possible in the case of Holmes. The compiler, therefore, has nothing new to offer the reader here, but
he has been at some pains to bring together all
the published information in regard to Thoreau's
writings which the works themselves offer and
which his biographers, and especially Mr. Sanborn, have given us. To these biographers, it is
needless to say, this book owes much of whatever
interest it may have.

The relation of Thoreau's more formal works
to his Journal is somewhat peculiar, and perhaps
demands a word of explanation in this Preface.
The Journal, begun in 1837 and continued until
within a few months of his death, was not merely
a chronicle of his daily doings: it was the record
of his daily thoughts also, and it contained the
first drafts of all his writings. The natural course
followed by each literary product was in the order
of journal entry, lecture, magazine article, and
book publication. Not every individual piece of
writing went through all the stages, but the beginning was always in the Journal. Of course the
Journal was not all used in this way: much of it

remained at his death still undrawn upon. Nor is the original draft of every one of his writings still to be seen, for Thoreau destroyed many pages of the Journal in the making of his books and essays. Enough is left, however, to show his methods of work, and readers may, with the help of the footnotes in the published Journal, readily compare for themselves the first drafts with the finished product, and learn the circumstances under which any given passage was originally written. The interrelations of the Works and the Journal are frequently noted in the pages of this bibliography.

October, 1908.

TABLE OF CONTENTS

NOTE ON THE FRONTISPIECE AND OTHER PORTRAITS OF THOREAU

THE portrait reproduced for the frontispiece of this volume is a daguerreotype hitherto unpublished, taken in June, 1856, by Benjamin D. Maxham of Worcester, Massachusetts. A comparison with the full-face portrait which has been reproduced so often as to have come to be the most familiar representation of Thoreau proves that the two daguerreotypes were taken at one sitting. The wrinkles in coat and waistcoat and the tying of the cravat are identical, though the hair is somewhat smoother in this new one, and pose and expression are different. This is the daguerreotype sent by Thoreau to Calvin H. Greene of Rochester, Michigan, in 1856. It was accompanied by the following letter, which is reproduced in facsimile herewith: —

CONCORD Saturday
June 21st '56.

DEAR SIR

On the 12 ult¹ I forwarded the two books to California, observing your directions in every particular, and I trust that Uncle Sam will discharge his duty faithfully. While in Worcester this week I obtained the accompanying daguerreotype, which my friends think is pretty good, though better looking than I.

¹ Thoreau habitually wrote "ult." for "inst." when referring to an earlier day in the current month. (See Editor's Preface to the *Journal*.)

Books & postage $2.64
 Daguerreotype 50
 Postage 16
             3.30
 5.00 You will accordingly
 3.30
find 1.70 enclosed with my shadow.
     Yrs.
      HENRY D. THOREAU.

Thoreau's correspondence with Greene was
first printed in "Some Unpublished Letters of
Henry D. and Sophia E. Thoreau," by Dr. Samuel A. Jones, to whose kindness the compiler of
this Bibliography is indebted for the privilege
of reproducing the daguerreotype and the letter,
both of which are now in Dr. Jones's possession.
That volume also gives some account of the circumstances attending the transmission of the
daguerreotype. It seems that Greene had asked
Thoreau for his picture, and had also ordered copies of the "Week" and "Walden" sent to his brother in California. Having heard that Thoreau
was poor, he enclosed five dollars and requested
him to keep the balance "for his trouble"! The
change, however, came back with the picture.

Besides this one there appear to be five portraits of Thoreau from the life, — two other
daguerreotypes taken at the same sitting, in June,
1856; a crayon drawing by Samuel W. Rowse,
made in 1854 and now hung in the Concord Public Library; and two ambrotypes taken by Dun-

shee in New Bedford for Mr. Daniel Ricketson in August, 1861. From one of these last and from personal recollection Mr. Walton Ricketson made an excellent medallion in profile, which has been reproduced in the "Familiar Letters" and elsewhere. The medallion deserves to rank with the original portraits, for Mr. Ricketson knew Thoreau well and seems to have been very successful in getting a likeness. Mr. Sanborn says that "it alone of the four likenesses extant shows the aquiline features as his comrades of the wood and mountain saw them, — not weakened by any effort to bring him to the standard of other men in garb or expression."

The daguerreotypes were taken during one of Thoreau's visits to Worcester, at the instance of his friends H. G. O. Blake and Theo. Brown. So far as can now be ascertained, but three were taken, two of which went to the Worcester friends, while the third was sent to Mr. Greene. Mr. Blake's has been reproduced a number of times, and is probably the only one published hitherto. It is now in the possession of Mr. Edward Harlow Russell of Worcester. Mr. Brown's is now owned by his son, Mr. William T. Brown of the same city, through whose kindness the writer has been permitted to examine it. It is practically identical in appearance with the Blake negative.

The Dunshee ambrotype — the two are so nearly identical in pose, expression, and detail that they may be treated as one — deserves to be better known than it is. It has only once been satisfac-

torily reproduced, however. That was in "Daniel
Ricketson and his Friends," where it appeared
in photogravure. The portrait pleased Thoreau's
family greatly. In sending it to Miss Thoreau
soon after the death of her brother, Mr. Ricketson
wrote: "When I heard of your brother's death, I
went to the artist who took the picture and got
a duplicate of the one I had for you. I send you
the strongest impression, the first taken. The one
I keep is a little lighter in color, which led me to
choose it, but I now see the stronger expression
in yours. If you were here, I should like for you
to take your choice. We all consider it very life-
like and one of the most successful likenesses we
ever saw. What is rather remarkable is that it
shows scarcely at all Henry's loss of health, suf-
fering deeply as he was at the time it was taken,
from his disease." ·Miss Thoreau wrote in reply:
"Until a few weeks since I did not know that
Henry had his picture taken when in New Bedford
last; he accidentally spoke of it, and said that
you considered it a good likeness. None of his
daguerreotypes have pleased us, and I did not im-
agine that the ambrotype would afford us much
satisfaction; still I felt curious to see it, thinking
I might get a copy of yours in case we liked it.
I need not tell you, for I cannot, how agreeably
surprised I was on opening the little box, to find
my own lost brother again. I could not restrain
my tears. I discover a slight shade about the eyes
expressive of weariness, but a stranger might not
observe it. I am very glad to possess a picture of

so late a date. The crayon drawn eight years ago
this summer we considered good; it betrays the
poet. I always liked it. Mr. Channing, Emerson,
Alcott, and many other friends who have looked at
the ambrotype express much satisfaction."

There are tintypes in existence taken from this
ambrotype and passing for original portraits of
Thoreau. The writer has not learned who is
responsible for them. Mr. Walton Ricketson
writes that he has no knowledge of them, and that
but two ambrotypes were made in New Bedford,
one of which is in his possession, while the other
was the one sent by his father to Miss Sophia
Thoreau. The latter is now in the collection of
the Concord Antiquarian Society. Mr. Ricketson
also states that two exposures were made at the
sitting, Dunshee retaining one negative and turn-
ing the other over to Mr. Daniel Ricketson. The
first negative was the one afterwards sent to Miss
Thoreau. So that both of the ambrotypes are
original portraits, taken directly from the sitter.[1]

In discussing the portraits of Thoreau, mention
must also be made of a full bust by Mr. Walton
Ricketson, which was reproduced in photogravure
in "Daniel Ricketson and his Friends," and of
a crude but amusing pencil sketch made by Mr.
Daniel Ricketson and reproduced in the same

---

[1] In the pages of this Bibliography, portraits are frequently described
as "the Maxham daguerreotype," "the Dunshee ambrotype," etc. Reference in the former case is usually, if not always, to Mr. Blake's daguerreotype; where an ambrotype is mentioned, the Concord ambrotype is to be
understood, except in the case of the one reproduced in *Daniel Ricketson
and his Friends*.

volume. This sketch was inscribed, "H. D. Thoreau as he presented himself at the door of Brooklawn, Dec. 25th, 1854. Age 37," and it represents Thoreau with hat, umbrella, and travelling-bag, as he appeared in making his first visit to Ricketson in New Bedford. It is not, of course, a serious attempt at portraiture. The bust was evidently modelled after the Rowse crayon, and represents the younger Thoreau, the Thoreau whom the sculptor, then only a boy, first met at his father's house, but with even more of youthful vigor than was his at that time. It is a conception of Thoreau the poet, and is naturally a somewhat idealized portrait.

The fact that the familiar daguerreotype has sometimes been reproduced without reversing — thus showing the subject as he appeared in his mirror but not precisely as his friends saw him — has given rise to the belief that two daguerreotypes have been reproduced, but the writer has been unable to find more than the one portrait, reproduced directly or reversed as the case might be. It is therefore a peculiar pleasure to be able to publish for the first time this portrait which has hitherto been unknown to most readers and admirers of Thoreau.

THOREAU'S BOOKS

BIBLIOGRAPHY OF THOREAU

A WEEK ON THE CONCORD AND MERRIMACK RIVERS

A WEEK | ON THE | CONCORD AND MERRIMACK RIVERS. | By | Henry D. Thoreau. | Boston and Cambridge: | *James Munroe and Company.* | New York: *George P. Putnam.* Philadelphia: *Lindsay* | *and Blackiston.* London: *John Chapman.* | 1849.

12mo, pp. 413. Collation: 1, title; 2, copyright and imprint (*Thurston, Torry and Company,* Boston, 31 Devonshire Street); 3, four lines of verse; 4, four lines of verse; 5, eight lines of verse; 6, blank; 7–14, "Concord River;" 15, half-title with motto; 16, blank; 17–44, "Saturday;" 45, half-title with motto; 46, motto; 47–120, "Sunday;" 121, half-title with motto; 122, motto; 123–185, "Monday;" 186, blank; 187, half-title with motto; 188, blank; 189–246, "Tuesday;" 247, half-title with motto; 248, blank; 249–311, "Wednesday;" 312, blank; 313, half-title with motto; 314, blank; 315–350, "Thursday;" 351, half-title with motto; 352, motto; 353–413, "Friday;" blank; advertisement: "Will soon be published, Walden, or Life in the Woods. By Henry D. Thoreau."

The book is bound in cloth and lettered in gilt on back *A Week* | *on the* | *Concord and* | *Merrimack* | *Rivers* | *Munroe & Co.*

A thousand copies were printed at the author's risk. Of these 75 were given away and 219 sold by Munroe, and the remaining 706 returned, October 28, 1853, to the author, who succeeded in disposing of a few of them himself. Thoreau's account of his receipt of the unsold remainder has often been quoted, but for completeness' sake should be reprinted here. The Journal for October 28, 1853, contains the following entry: —

"For a year or two past, my *publisher*, falsely so called, has been writing from time to time to ask what disposition should be made of the copies of 'A Week on the Concord and Merrimack Rivers' still on hand, and at last suggesting that he had use for the room they occupied in his cellar. So I had them all sent to me here, and they arrived to-day by express, filling the man's wagon, — 706 copies out of an edition of 1000 which I bought of Munroe four years ago and have been ever since paying for, and have not quite paid for yet. The wares are sent to me at last, and I have an opportunity to examine my purchase. They are something more substantial than fame, as my back knows, which has borne them up two flights of stairs to a place similar to that to which they trace their origin. Of the remaining two hundred and ninety odd, seventy-five were given away, the rest sold. I have now a library of nearly nine hundred volumes, over seven hundred of which I wrote myself. Is it not well that the author should behold the fruits of his labor? My works are piled up on one side of my chamber half as high as my head, my *opera omnia*. This is authorship; these are the work of my brain. There was just one piece of good luck in the venture. The unbound were tied up by the printer four years ago in stout wrappers, and inscribed, —

H. D. THOREAU's
Concord River
50 cops.

So Munroe had only to cross out 'River' and write 'Mass.' and deliver them to the expressman at once. I can see now what I write for, the result of my labors.

"Nevertheless, in spite of this result, sitting beside the inert mass of my works, I take up my pen to-night to record what thought or experience I may have had, with as much satisfaction as ever. Indeed, I believe that this result is more inspiring and better for me than if a thousand had bought my wares. It affects my privacy less and leaves me freer."

Under date of November 20, 1853, he records how at one time he had considered speculating in cranberries as a means of raising money to pay his debt to Munroe. The settlement was finally made November 28 and he then placed twelve copies of the *Week* with Munroe on sale. He goes on to say: "I have paid him directly out of pocket since the book was published two hundred and ninety dollars and taken his receipt for it. This does not include postage on proof-sheets, etc., etc. I have received from other quarters about fifteen dollars. This has been the pecuniary value of the book." A memorandum in the Journal states that he "sent Fields 12 copies of the *Week*, Oct. 18th, '54," a little over two months after the publication of *Walden*. It was not until 1862, however, that Ticknor & Fields put their imprint on the book, as appears in the next title. Meanwhile Thoreau continued to sell the book from time to time from the stock he had carried into his attic. A copy recently sold in New York for $60 was originally bought from Thoreau by Miss Sarah E. Sanborn in April, 1855, for $1.25. The demand was slight, however, and but few copies were thus disposed of.

By a blunder in the printing-office three lines were dropped out at the bottom of page 396. Thoreau wrote in the missing lines in pencil whenever he sold a copy of the book, and a number of such copies are in existence. The bulk of the edition, however, both those bearing the date 1849 and those with the 1862 title-page, lack this correction.

A Week on the Concord and Merrimack Rivers was made up largely — probably almost entirely — from Thoreau's Journal from the period of his earliest journalizing in 1837 up to the time of the completion of the manuscript, which was probably in 1847. Many Journal passages used in writing the book are printed in the *Journal* as issued in the Walden Edition and indicated there by footnotes, but the great bulk of them were destroyed by Thoreau in the making of the book. Many of the poems appearing in the *Week* and a few prose essays embodied therein had first found publication in *The Dial*, and these will be found noted in the list of *Dial* articles and poems on pp. 64–68.

It was long after the *Week* was completed before Thoreau

found a publisher for it, but he appears to have made certain emendations in it in the interval. The essay on Friendship incorporated in the ":Wednesday" chapter was added at this time, as appears from an entry in Mr. Alcott's diary under date of January 13, 1848, where he says that Thoreau had that day read him an essay on Friendship which he had just written.[1]

Among the most interesting copies extant of this first edition of the *Week* are those in the possession of Mr. Stephen H. Wakeman of New York. They include the copies once belonging to William Cullen Bryant, Nathaniel Hawthorne, H. G. O. Blake, and Ellery Channing, — the last very fully annotated by that most intimate friend of Thoreau's. Mr. Paul Lemperly of Cleveland, Ohio, owns a copy bearing the author's inscription to his sister and containing corrections by Thoreau and notes by Sophia Thoreau.

A WEEK | ON THE | CONCORD AND MERRIMACK RIVERS. | By | Henry D. Thoreau, | Author of "Walden." | Boston : | *Ticknor and Fields.* | 1862.
16mo, pp. 413.

The copies with this title-page are of the first edition, rebound. The binders omitted to remove the leaf announcing the future publication of *Walden*. An article by Dr. S. A. Jones telling the story of these volumes in a playful way appeared in *The Inlander*, a magazine published by the students of the University of Michigan, and is quoted by Dr. Jones in his Bibliography of Thoreau.

A WEEK | ON THE | CONCORD AND MERRIMACK RIVERS. | By Henry D. Thoreau, | Author of "Walden," etc. | New and Revised Edition. | [*Device*] | Boston : | *Ticknor and Fields.* | 1868 [1867].
16mo, pp. 415.

The first 8 pages are front matter; p. 1 is a half-title

[1] F. B. Sanborn, *Thoreau*, p. 304.

and p. 2 a list of Thoreau's books. On p. 8 appears for
the first time a quotation of four lines from Ovid, with
a translation. There are also two new quotations from
the Robin Hood Ballads on the "Monday" half-title
and its back. This edition was printed from new plates.
It contains two unfortunate misprints, — "souls" for
"stools," p. 273, third line from bottom, and "interrupt"
for "interpret," p. 414, line 12, — which persisted in
the Riverside Edition, but were corrected in the Manuscript and Walden editions. Later impressions of this
edition were issued in 12mo size. See Addenda.

A WEEK ON THE CONCORD | AND MERRIMAC
[*sic*] RIVERS, | By Henry Thoreau : With | a
Prefatory Note by | Will H. Dircks. | London : |
Walter Scott, 24 Warwick Lane. | Toronto :
W. J. Gage & Co. [1889.]
Square 16mo, pp. xx, 349. In the Camelot
series.

Though "Merrimac" is the common way of spelling the
name of the river at the present day, the American editions of
the book have always preserved Thoreau's old-fashioned spelling of it.

THE SAME. With a Prefatory Note by Will H.
Dircks. London : *Walter Scott Limited.* [1895.]
16mo, pp. xx, 349. Electrogravure frontispiece, Thoreau's Cove.

A WEEK ON THE CONCORD | AND MERRIMACK |
RIVERS. | By | Henry David Thoreau | [*Device*] |
Boston and New York | *Houghton, Mifflin
and Company* | The Riverside Press, Cam-
bridge | MDCCCXCIV [1893].
Crown 8vo, pp. xviii, 531. Vol. i of the Riverside Edition. With Publishers' Advertisement

to the edition (2 pp.), Introductory Note (9
pp.), Table of Poetical Quotations, index, and
photogravure frontispiece from the Rowse
crayon portrait of 1854.

A WEEK ON THE CONCORD | AND MERRIMACK
RIVERS | By Henry David Thoreau | Cam-
bridge | *Printed at the Riverside Press* | 1894
[1893].
    8vo, pp. xviii, 531. Volume i of the Large-
Paper Edition. Portrait by Rowse.

Limited edition of 150 copies printed from the plates
of the Riverside Edition and issued at the same time.

THE SAME. With an Introduction by Nathan
H. Dole. New York: *Thomas Y. Crowell &
Co.* [1900.]
    16mo and 12mo, pp. xxiv, 399. With illus-
trations.

Issued in several styles.

THE WRITINGS OF | HENRY DAVID THOREAU |
A WEEK ON THE | CONCORD AND MERRIMACK |
RIVERS | [*Device*] | Boston and New York |
Houghton Mifflin and Company | MDCCCCVI.
    8vo, pp. xlviii, 435. Vol. i of the Manu-
script Edition, limited to 600 copies. With
Biographical Sketch by R. W. Emerson, Introductory Note, portrait, and five photogravure illustrations from photographs by
Herbert W. Gleason. Collation; i, half-title;
ii, number of set, with autograph signature of
the publishers; iii, title; iv, copyright; v–vii,
Publishers' Advertisement to the Manuscript

Edition of Thoreau's Writings; viii, blank; ix–xi, contents; xii, blank; xiii, list of illustrations; xiv, blank; xv–xl, Biographical Sketch; xli–xlvii, Introductory Note; xlviii, blank; 1, half-title; 2, poetical mottoes; 3–420, text; 421, half-title; 422, blank; 423–427, Table of Poetical Quotations; 428, blank; 429–435, index; [436], printers' imprint, "The Riverside Press," etc.

The frontispiece portrait is a photogravure of the Maxham daguerreotype. Immediately before it is inserted a piece of Thoreau's manuscript. See also description of this edition on pp. 52, 53.

THE SAME. Boston and New York: *Houghton, Mifflin & Co.* 1906.

12mo, pp. xlviii, 435. Vol. i of the Walden Edition. With Biographical Sketch by R. W. Emerson, Introductory Note, portrait, and five photogravure illustrations from photographs by Herbert W. Gleason. Collation: i, half-title; ii, blank; iii, title; iv, copyright; v–vii, Publishers' Advertisement to the Walden Edition; otherwise as in Manuscript Edition.

The illustrations are as in the Manuscript Edition, but the manuscript is omitted. Printed from the plates of the Manuscript Edition.

WALDEN

WALDEN; | OR, | LIFE IN THE WOODS. | By Henry D. Thoreau, | Author of "A Week on the Concord and Merrimack Rivers." | [*Cut of*

Thoreau's hut at Walden Pond] | [*Motto*] |
Boston: *Ticknor and Fields.* | MDCCCLIV.
16mo, pp. 357. Map of Walden Pond facing
p. 307. Collation: 1, title; 2, copyright and
imprint (Stereotyped at the Boston Stereotype
Foundry); 3, contents; 4, blank; 5–357, text.

On p. 87, following the first chapter, are lines from
T. Carew headed "Complemental Verses." (The dates
of the advertisements at the end of the book cannot
be regarded as of serious importance. At a recent sale,
however, a copy having advertising dated April, 1854,
brought a much higher price than one with advertising
dated May, 1854, and this in spite of the fact that the
book itself was not published till August of that year!)
The book was bound in cloth and lettered on back
Walden | Life in the Woods | Thoreau | Ticknor & Co.

Walden, like the *Week,* was written largely if not
almost entirely in Thoreau's Journal before it was made
into a book, and the writing was by no means confined
to the years he spent on the shore of Walden Pond,
though the bulk of it was done there. The Journal
entries incorporated in *Walden* date from at least as far
back as 1839 and extend to within a few months of the
publication of the book. Many of them are to be found
in the *Journal* as published, but most of them, especially
of those belonging to the Walden period, were destroyed
in making the copy for the book. The lines beginning
"Light-winged Smoke, Icarian bird" were published
in *The Dial* for April, 1843, under the title of "Smoke,"
but nothing else in the book appears ever to have been
printed before.

Walden was published August 9, 1854. The first reprinting seems to have been in 1864.

Mr. Paul Lemperly of Cleveland, Ohio, has in his
possession a copy of *Walden* formerly belonging to

Thoreau himself, which contains many interesting corrections and annotations made by the author. Several
transcripts of these notes are in existence. Dr. S. A. Jones
and Mr. E. B. Hill have copies, and there is another in
the office of Houghton Mifflin Company. Such of these
corrections as are merely typographical have been embodied in the latest impression of the Riverside Edition
of *Walden*. Among these is the alteration of the word
"post" to "port" on page 24 (Riv. Ed. p. 35). Of the
other annotations, two of the most important from the
point of view of natural history are the correction of "single
spruce" to "double spruce" on page 137 and of "white
spruce" to "black spruce" on page 217.

WALDEN. Edinburgh: *David Douglas*. London:
Hamilton, Adams & Co. 1884.

Post 8vo, pp. 357.

This edition, which, as nearly as can be judged from the
evidence at the compiler's command, was issued under
the joint imprint indicated above, is doubtless simply
the American edition with a new title-page. It was published in April, 1884, and was the first edition of *Walden*
to appear under an English imprint.

THE SAME. | With an Introductory Note by Will
H. Dircks. London: *Walter Scott*, 24 Warwick
Lane, Paternoster Row. 1886.

Square 16mo, pp. xxviii, 336. In the Camelot Classics, edited by Ernest Rhys.

The first original English edition. An appendix gives
a selection from the *Week* and three of Thoreau's poems.

THE SAME. With an Introductory Note by Will
H. Dircks. London: *Walter Scott*. Toronto:
W. J. Gage & Co. 1888.

Square 16mo. Printed from the same plates
as the 1886 London edition.

THE SAME. In the Riverside Aldine Series. Boston: *Houghton, Mifflin & Co.* 1889.

2 vols. 16mo, pp. 1–259, [i–vi], 261–514.

The first six pages of vol. i are made up of front matter. A small first edition was issued with uncut edges and paper label.

WALDEN | OR, LIFE IN THE WOODS | By | Henry David Thoreau | [*Motto*] | [*Device*] | Boston and New York | *Houghton, Mifflin and Company* | The Riverside Press, Cambridge | MDCCCXCIV [1893].

Crown 8vo, pp. i–viii, 7–522. Vol. II of the Riverside Edition. With Introductory Note (2 pp.) and index.

The text is printed from the plates of the Riverside Edition.

WALDEN | OR, | LIFE IN THE WOODS | By | Henry D. Thoreau | [*Motto*] | Cambridge | Printed at the Riverside Press | 1894 [1893].

8vo, pp. i–viii, 7–522. Vol. II of the Large-Paper Edition.

A limited edition of 150 copies printed from the plates of the Riverside Edition and issued at the same time.

THE SAME. With an Introductory Note by Will H. Dircks. London: *Walter Scott Limited.* [1895.]

16mo, pp. xxx, 336. Electrogravure frontispiece, Walden Pond.

WALDEN | By | Henry D. Thoreau | With an Introduction by Bradford Torrey | Illustrated with Photogravures | In Two Volumes | I [II] |

[*Device*] | Boston and New York | *Houghton, Mifflin and Company* | The Riverside Press, Cambridge | MDCCCXCVII.

12mo, pp. i–xliv, 7–259; i–vi, 261–522. 31 full-page illustrations.

Known as the Holiday Edition. The text is printed from the plates of the Riverside Edition. It was published in London with a new title-page bearing imprint of Gay & Bird, 1897.

WALDEN; OR, LIFE IN THE WOODS. By Henry David Thoreau. With a Biographical Sketch by Ralph Waldo Emerson. Boston: *Houghton, Mifflin & Co.* [1897.]

Crown 8vo, pp. xxxviii, 7–522. Popular Edition.

Printed from the plates of the Riverside Edition with the Emerson Biographical Sketch prefixed.

THE SAME. In Cambridge Classics. Boston: *Houghton, Mifflin & Co.* [1898.]

Identical with the Popular Edition except in binding.

WALDEN. With an Introduction by Charles G. D. Roberts. New York: *T. Y. Crowell & Company.* [1899.]

16mo and 12mo, pp. xvi, 350. With illustrations.

Issued in several styles.

WALDEN | By Henry David Thoreau | With an Introduction | by Bradford Torrey | Illustrated with Photogravures | [*Device*] | Boston and New York | *Houghton, Mifflin and Company* | The Riverside Press, Cambridge | 1902.

12mo, pp. xliv, 7–522.

A new "Holiday Edition" in one volume with the illustrations of the two-volume edition and printed from the same plates. It was published in London with a new title-page bearing imprint of Gay & Bird, 1902.

WALDEN: MY LIFE IN THE WOODS. London: *Arthur C. Fifield*, Simple Life Press. 1904.

16mo, paper, pp. 158. Abridged edition, with portrait and cut of Thoreau's Walden hermitage from a sketch by Miss May Alcott (not by *Mr.* Alcott, as stated, and not unpublished; see p. 90).

Published at sixpence. There is also a shilling edition from the same plates with three more illustrations.

THE WRITINGS OF | HENRY DAVID THOREAU | WALDEN | [*Device*] | Boston and New York | *Houghton Mifflin and Company* | MDCCCCVI.

8vo, pp. x, 375. Vol. II of the Manuscript Edition, limited to 600 copies. With Introductory Note and five photogravure illustrations from photographs by Herbert W. Gleason. Collation: i, half-title; ii, number of set; iii, title; iv, copyright; v, contents; vi, blank; vii, list of illustrations; viii, blank; ix, x, Introductory Note; 1, half-title; 2, blank; 3–367, text; 368, blank; 369–375, index; [376], printers' imprint.

See also description of this edition on pp. 52, 53.

THE SAME. Boston and New York: *Houghton, Mifflin & Co.* 1906.

12mo, pp. x, 375. Vol. II of the Walden Edition. With Introductory Note and five photogravure illustrations from photographs by Herbert W. Gleason. Collation: i, half-title; ii, blank; otherwise as in Manuscript Edition.

Printed from the plates of the Manuscript Edition and with the same illustrations.

WALDEN, OR LIFE IN THE WOODS. With an Introduction by Theodore Watts-Dunton. London: *Henry Frowde*, Oxford University Press. [1906.]

18mo, pp. xvi, 299. In the World's Classics.

WALDEN. With an Introduction by Richard Whiteing. London: *Blackie & Son*. [1906.]

18mo, pp. xii, 410.

THE SAME. With an Introductory Essay on Thoreau by R. W. Emerson. London: *George Routledge & Sons*.

Crown 8vo, pp. 256.

TRANSLATIONS

WALDEN, Deutsch von Emma Emmerich. München: Verlag Concord [*J. Palm*]. 1897.

Cr. 8vo, pp. xxii, 356.

Catalogued in Kayser's Neues Bücher-Lexicon. The Verlag Concord, named after Thoreau's birthplace ("*nach dem Geburtsort Thoreaus benannt*"), is now located in Stettin, Prussia, under the management of Otto Carius.

HENRY D. THOREAU | WALDEN | ODER LEBEN IN DEN WÄLDERN | Mit Porträt | [*Device*] | [*Rule*] | Verlegt bei *Eugen Diederichs* | Jena und Leipzig. 1905.

Crown 8vo, pp. xxiv, 341. On title-back: "Aus dem Englischen übersetzt von Wilhelm Nobbe."

The portrait is a reproduction of the ambrotype. There are a 24-page biographical sketch and 8 pages of notes. The biographical sketch is dated St. Louis, Mo., Januar, 1905, and signed Wilhelm Nobbe.

EXCURSIONS

EXCURSIONS. | By | Henry D. Thoreau. | Author of "Walden," and "A Week on the Concord and | Merrimack Rivers." | [*Device*] | Boston: *Ticknor and Fields.* | 1863.

16mo, pp. 319; steel portrait. Collation of front matter: 1, blank; 2, advertisement of Thoreau's Writings; 3, title; 4, copyright and imprint (Riverside, Cambridge: Stereotyped and printed by H. O. Houghton); 5, contents; 6, blank.

CONTENTS:—

Biographical Sketch, by R. W. Emerson, 7–34.
Natural History of Massachusetts, 37–72.
A Walk to Wachusett, 73–96.
The Landlord, 97–108.
A Winter Walk, 109–134.
The Succession of Forest Trees, 135–160.
Walking, 161–214.
Autumnal Tints, 215–265.
Wild Apples, 266–306.
Night and Moonlight, 307–319.

Pages 35 and 36 are the half-title " Excursions " and its blank back. The portrait is from Rowse's crayon. The book was bound in cloth and lettered on back *Excursions* | *by* | *H. D.* | *Thoreau.* | *Author of* | *Walden* | *and* | *A Week on* | *Concord* | *River.* | *Ticknor & Co.*

Excursions was formerly often listed under the title of "Excursions in Field and Forest." The last four words were merely explanatory, however, and never appeared on the title-page. The papers composing the book were collected by Miss Sophia E. Thoreau from various sources. "Natural History of Massachusetts" and "A Winter Walk" first appeared in *The Dial,* "A Walk to Wachusett" in the *Boston Miscellany*, "The Landlord" in the *Democratic Review*, "The Succession of Forest Trees" in the *New York Tribune*, and "Walking," "Autumnal Tints," "Wild Apples," and "Night and Moonlight" in the *Atlantic Monthly*.

EXCURSIONS | By | Henry David Thoreau | [*Device*] | Boston and New York | *Houghton, Mifflin and Company* | The Riverside Press, Cambridge | MDCCCXCIV [1893].

Crown 8vo, pp. x, 472. Vol. IX of the Riverside Edition. With Introductory Note (4 pp.) and index.

CONTENTS : —

A Yankee in Canada.
Natural History of Massachusetts.
The Landlord.
A Winter Walk.
A Walk to Wachusett.
The Succession of Forest Trees.
Walking.
Autumnal Tints.
Wild Apples.
Night and Moonlight.
May Days.
Days and Nights in Concord.

It will be noticed that this book differs materially in contents from the book originally published under this title. The Biographical Sketch is omitted (transferred to the volume entitled *Miscellanies*), and the long narrative of the Canadian excursion and two papers composed of extracts from Thoreau's Journal are added. These last papers had been printed in the *Atlantic* and *Scribner's* respectively. "A Yankee in Canada" had formerly been published in a volume with Anti-Slavery and Reform Papers.

EXCURSIONS | By | Henry David Thoreau | Cambridge | Printed at the Riverside Press | 1894 [1893].

8vo, pp. x, 472. Vol. IX of the Large-Paper Edition.

A limited edition of 150 copies printed from the plates of the Riverside Edition and issued at the same time.

THE MAINE WOODS

THE MAINE WOODS | By Henry D. Thoreau, | Author of "A Week on the Concord and Merrimack Rivers," | "Walden," "Excursions," etc., etc. | Boston: | *Ticknor and Fields.* | 1864.

16mo, pp. [vi], 328. Collation: List of Thoreau's Writings; [i], title; [ii], copyright and imprint (University Press: Welch, Bigelow, and Company, Cambridge); [iii], [note]; [iv], blank; [v], contents; [vi], blank; 1–304, text; 305, half-title; 306, blank; 307–328, Appendix. 23 pages of advertising at end.

CONTENTS:—

Ktaadn, pp. 1–84.
Chesuncook, pp. 85–160.
The Allegash and East Branch, pp. 161–304.
Appendix: —
    I. Trees, pp. 307, 308.
    II. Flowers and Shrubs, pp. 308–311.
    III. List of Plants, pp. 312–320.
    IV. List of Birds, pp. 321, 322.
    V. Quadrupeds, p. 322.
    VI. Outfit for an Excursion, pp. 322, 323.
    VII. A List of Indian Words, pp. 324–328.

Edited jointly by Sophia E. Thoreau and William Ellery Channing. The note on p. [iii] reads: —

"The first of the papers following was published in 'The Union Magazine' (New York), in 1848; the second, 'Chesuncook,' came out in the 'Atlantic Monthly,' in 1858; and the last is now for the first time printed."

The book was bound in cloth, and lettered on back *The | Maine | Woods | by | Thoreau. | Author of | Walden | and | A Week on | Concord | River | Ticknor & Co.*

The paper entitled "The Allegash and East Branch," as well as the Appendix, was not entirely prepared for the press until after the author's death, and it suffers from careless editing.

THE MAINE WOODS | By | Henry David Thoreau | [*Device*] | Boston and New York | *Houghton, Mifflin and Company* | The Riverside Press, Cambridge | MDCCCXCIV [1893].

Crown 8vo, pp. x, 442. Vol. III of the Riverside Edition. With Introductory Note (4 pp.), Appendix (27 pp.), and Index.

THE MAINE WOODS | By | Henry David Thoreau | Cambridge | Printed at the Riverside Press | 1894 [1893].

8vo, pp. x, 442. Vol. III of the Large-Paper Edition.

A limited edition of 150 copies printed from the plates of the Riverside Edition and issued at the same time.

THE WRITINGS OF | HENRY DAVID THOREAU | THE MAINE WOODS | [*Device*] | Boston and New York: | *Houghton Mifflin and Company* | MDCCCCVI.

8vo, pp. xii, 364. Vol. III of the Manuscript Edition, limited to 600 copies. With Introductory Note and five photogravure illustrations

from photographs by Herbert W. Gleason.
Collation: i, half-title; ii, number of set; iii,
title; iv, copyright; v, contents; vi, blank; vii,
list of illustrations; viii, blank; ix–xi, Introductory Note; xii, blank; 1, half-title; 2, blank;
3–327, text; 328, blank; 329–357, appendix;
358, blank; 359–364, index; [365], blank; [366],
printer's imprint.

See also description of this edition on pp. 52, 53.

THE SAME. Boston and New York: *Houghton,
Mifflin & Co.* 1906.

12mo, pp. xii, 364. Vol. III of the Walden
Edition. With Introductory Note and five
photogravure illustrations from photographs
by Herbert W. Gleason. Collation as in Manuscript Edition except that p. ii is blank.

Printed from the plates of the Manuscript Edition and
having the same illustrations.

THE SAME. With an Introduction by Annie
Russell Marble. New York: *Thomas Y.
Crowell & Co.* [1906.]

16mo and 12mo, pp. xvi, 359. With illustrations.

Issued in several styles.

CAPE COD

CAPE COD. | By | Henry D. Thoreau, | Author of
"A Week on the Concord and Merrimack
Rivers," | "Walden," "Excursions," "The
Maine Woods," | etc., etc. | [*Motto*] | [*Device*] |
Boston: | *Ticknor and Fields.* | 1865 [1864].

16mo, pp. [iv], 252. Collation: A list of Thoreau's writings; [i], title; [ii], copyright and imprint (University Press: Welch, Bigelow, and Company, Cambridge); [iii], contents; [iv], blank; 1–252, text; 24 pages of advertising.

Edited by Sophia E. Thoreau and William Ellery Channing.

CONTENTS: —

The Shipwreck.
Stage-coach Views.
The Plains of Nauset.
The Beach.
The Wellfleet Oysterman.
The Beach Again.
Across the Cape.
The Highland Light.
The Sea and the Desert.
Provincetown.

The first four chapters were published by their author in *Putnam's Magazine* in 1855. The fifth and eighth appeared in the *Atlantic Monthly* in October and December, 1864. The book was bound in cloth and lettered on back *Cape | Cod | by | Thoreau. | Author of | Walden | and | A Week on | Concord | River | Ticknor & Co.*

An edition from the same plates was published in London, June 1, 1865, by Sampson Low, Son & Marston. It appears to have been the first edition of any of Thoreau's books to be issued under a foreign imprint.

CAPE COD. | By | Henry David Thoreau | [*Motto*] [*Device*] | Boston and New York | *Houghton, Mifflin and Company* | The Riverside Press, Cambridge | MDCCCXCIV [1889].

Crown 8vo, pp. viii, 336. Vol. IV of the

Riverside Edition. With Introductory Note (1 p.) and index.

CAPE COD | By | Henry David Thoreau | Cambridge | Printed at the Riverside Press | 1894 [1893].

8vo, pp. viii, 336. Vol. IV of the Large-Paper Edition, limited to 150 copies.

Printed from the plates of the Riverside Edition and issued at the same time.

CAPE COD | By | Henry David Thoreau | With Illustrations from Sketches | in Colors by Amelia M. Watson | In Two Volumes | I [II] | [*Device*] | Boston and New York | *Houghton, Mifflin and Company* | The Riverside Press, Cambridge | MDCCCXCVI.

Crown 8vo, pp. i–viii, 1–173; 1–208. Frontispieces and many marginal illustrations.

THE SAME. With an Introduction by Annie Russell Marble. New York: *Thomas Y. Crowell & Co.* [1907.]

16mo and 12mo, pp. xiv, 263. With illustrations.

Issued in several styles.

LETTERS TO VARIOUS PERSONS

LETTERS | TO VARIOUS PERSONS. | By | Henry D. Thoreau, | Author of "A Week on the Concord and Merrimack Rivers," | "Walden," etc., etc. | [*Device*] | Boston: | *Ticknor and Fields.* | 1865.

16mo, pp. [vi], 229. Collation: List of Thoreau's Writings; [i], title; [ii], copyright and imprint (University Press: Welch, Bigelow & Co., Cambridge); [iii], Editor's Notice, signed R. W. E., 12 May, 1865; [iv], blank; [v], contents; [vi], blank; 1–207, Letters; 208, blank; 209, half-title; 210, blank; 211–229, Poems.

The Editor's Note reads: —

"It may interest the reader of this book to know that nearly all these letters have been printed directly from the original autographs furnished by the persons to whom they were addressed. A few have been carefully copied, but without alteration, from the worn and torn originals. In some letters, passages have been omitted, on account of private or personal references. Otherwise, the letters have been printed as they stood, with very few verbal corrections."

The nine poems included are: —

Sympathy.
"Romans, Countrymen, and Lovers."
Inspiration.
The Fisher's Boy.
Mountains.
Smoke.
Smoke in Winter.
Mist.
Haze.

The book is bound in cloth, lettered on back *Letters | by | H. D. | Thoreau | Author of | Excursions | and | A Week on | Concord | River | Ticknor & Co.* The letters were collected and edited by Ralph Waldo Emerson.

A YANKEE IN CANADA, WITH ANTI-SLAVERY AND REFORM PAPERS

A | Yankee in Canada, | with | Anti-Slavery and Reform | Papers. | By | Henry D. Thoreau, | Author of "A Week on the Concord and

Merrimack Rivers," | "Walden," "Cape Cod,"
etc., etc. | [*Device*] | Boston: | *Ticknor and
Fields.* | 1866.

16mo, pp. [iv], 286. Collation: [i], title; [ii],
copyright and imprint (University Press:
Welch, Bigelow & Co., Cambridge); [iii],
contents; [iv], blank; 1, half-title and mottoes;
2, blank; 3–93, A Yankee in Canada; 94,
blank; 95, half-title; 96, blank; 97–286, Anti-
Slavery and Reform Papers.

CONTENTS: —

A Yankee in Canada.
  I. Concord to Montreal, pp. 3–18.
  II. Quebec and Montmorenci, pp. 18–36.
  III. St. Anne, pp. 37–63.
  IV. The Walls of Quebec, pp. 64–78.
  V. The Scenery of Quebec; and the River St. Lawrence,
     pp. 78–93.

The first three chapters appeared in *Putnam's Magazine*
under the title of "Excursion to Canada," but the later chapters were withdrawn by the author on account of a disagreement with the editor, George William Curtis. See page 71.

Anti-Slavery and Reform Papers.
  Slavery in Massachusetts, pp. 97–116. (An address de-
  livered at the Anti-slavery Convention at Framingham,
  Mass., July 4, 1854, and printed in *The Liberator* for
  July 21 of that year.)
  Prayers, pp. 117–122. (This article was ascribed to Thoreau by mistake, only the verses beginning "Great God,
  I ask thee for no meaner pelf" being his. The essay
  itself, which was printed in *The Dial*, was by Emerson
  and is now published in his posthumous volume *The
  Natural History of Intellect.*)
  Civil Disobedience, pp. 123–151. (First printed under
  the title of "Resistance to Civil Government" in *Æsthetic Papers*, edited by Miss Elizabeth P. Peabody,
  1849.)

A Plea for Captain John Brown, pp. 152–181. (This address was first printed in James Redpath's *Echoes of Harper's Ferry*, Boston, 1860. See also p. 74.)

Paradise (to be) Regained, pp. 182–205. (A review of a book by J. A. Etzler. It was first printed in *The Democratic Review* for November, 1843.)

Herald of Freedom, pp. 206–210. (A notice of the anti-slavery paper of that name; printed in *The Dial* for April, 1844.)

Thomas Carlyle and his Works, pp. 211–247. (From *Graham's Magazine*, March and April, 1847.)

Life without Principle, pp. 248–273. (Printed posthumously in the *Atlantic Monthly*, October, 1863.)

Wendell Phillips before the Concord Lyceum, pp. 274–277. (A letter published in *The Liberator*, March 28, 1845.)

The Last Days of John Brown, pp. 278–286. (Printed in *The Liberator* for July 27, 1860, as part of a report of a memorial meeting held at North Elba, N. Y., July 4, 1860, where this address was read by the Secretary.)

The book was bound in cloth, and lettered in gilt on back *A | Yankee | in | Canada | By | Thoreau. | Author of | Walden | and | A Week on | Concord | River | Ticknor & Co.*

EARLY SPRING IN MASSACHUSETTS

EARLY SPRING IN MASSACHUSETTS. | From the Journal of | Henry D. Thoreau, | Author of "A Week on the Concord and Merrimack Rivers," | "Walden," etc. | [*Motto*] | [*Device*] Boston: | *Houghton, Mifflin and Company.* | The Riverside Press, Cambridge. | 1881.

12mo, pp. viii, 318. Collation: i, title; ii, copyright and imprint; iii–vii, Introductory, signed H. G. O. Blake; viii, blank; 1–318, text.

Thoreau's sister Sophia, who inherited his manuscript journals, bequeathed them upon her death in October, 1876, to her brother's friend and correspondent, Harrison

G. O. Blake of Worcester, Mass. Mr. Blake wished to bring the thoughts imbedded in the Journal before the public, and judged that a selection from the abundance of material was the most practicable way to accomplish his end. His arrangement of the selections is explained in his introduction to this first volume that he compiled. "In reading the Journal for my own satisfaction, I had sometimes been wont to attend each day to what was written on the same day of the month in some other year; desiring thus to be led to notice, in my walks, the phenomena which Thoreau noticed, so to be brought nearer to the writer by observing the same sights, sounds, etc., and if possible have my love of nature quickened by him. This habit suggested the arrangement of dates in the following pages, viz., the bringing together of passages under the same day of the month in different years. In this way I hoped to make an interesting picture of the progress of the seasons, of Thoreau's year." This method of treating Thoreau's journals had been suggested some years earlier by Mr. Alcott in his *Concord Days* (1872).

EARLY SPRING | IN MASSACHUSETTS | From the Journal of | Henry David Thoreau | Edited by H. G. O. Blake | [*Motto*] | [*Device*] | Boston and New York | *Houghton, Mifflin and Company* | The Riverside Press, Cambridge | MDCCCXCIV [1893].

Crown 8vo, pp. x, 354. Vol. v of the Riverside Edition. With Introductory Note (5 pp.), signed H. G. O. Blake (with postscript signed H. G. O. B.), index, and frontispiece portrait reproduced in photogravure from the Maxham daguerreotype.

This edition contains matter covering the first four days of April, which had appeared in the *Atlantic Monthly*

in April, 1878, but had been omitted from the first edition
of the book.

THE SAME. Cambridge: Printed at the Riverside Press. 1894 [1893].

8vo, pp. x, 354. Vol. v of the Large-Paper
Edition.

A limited edition of 150 copies printed from the plates
of the Riverside Edition and issued simultaneously
with it.

SUMMER

SUMMER: From the Journal | of Henry D. Tho-
reau | Edited by H. G. O. Blake | [*Motto*] |
[*Device*] | Boston | *Houghton, Mifflin and
Company* | New York: 11 East Seventeenth
Street | The Riverside Press, Cambridge |
1884.

12mo, pp. vi, 382. With a map of Concord.
Collation: i, title; ii, copyright and printer's
imprint (The Riverside Press, Cambridge:
Electrotyped and Printed by H. .O Houghton
& Co.); iii–v, Introductory, signed The Editor
and dated Worcester, May, 1884; vi, blank;
1–372, text; 373–382, index.

The double-page map of Concord is inserted as a
frontispiece. A panel of advertising (list of Thoreau's
books) precedes the map, and there are 16 pages of advertising at the end of the book. The book follows the
plan of *Early Spring in Massachusetts* in its arrangement.

THE SAME. London: *T. Fisher Unwin.* 1884.

8vo, pp. vi, 382.

The American edition with a new title-page, published
in September, 1884.

SUMMER | From the Journal of | Henry David Thoreau | Edited by | H. G. O. Blake | [*Motto*] | [*Device*] | Boston and New York | *Houghton, Mifflin and Company* | The Riverside Press, Cambridge | MDCCCXCIV [1893].

Crown 8vo, pp. viii, 382. Vol. VI of the Riverside Edition. With Introductory Note (3 pp.) signed The Editor, index, and a map of Concord.

The text was printed from the plates of the first edition.

THE SAME. Cambridge: Printed at the Riverside Press. 1894 [1893].

8vo, pp. viii, 382. Vol. VI of the Large-Paper Edition.

A limited edition of 150 copies issued simultaneously with the Riverside Edition and printed from the same plates.

WINTER

WINTER: From the Journal | of Henry D. Thoreau | Edited by H. G. O. Blake | [*Motto*] [*Device*] | Boston and New York | *Houghton, Mifflin and Company* | The Riverside Press, Cambridge | 1888 [1887].

12mo, pp. vi, 439. Collation: i, title; ii, copyright and printer's imprint; iii–vi, Introductory, signed The Editor; 1–430, text; 431–439, index.

WINTER | From the Journal of | Henry David Thoreau | Edited by | H. G. O. Blake | [*Motto*] | [*Device*] | Boston and New York | *Houghton, Mifflin and Company* | The Riverside Press, Cambridge | MDCCCXCIV [1893].

Crown 8vo, pp. viii, 439. Vol. VIII of the Riverside Edition. With Introductory Note (4 pp.) signed The Editor, and index.

Printed from the plates of the first edition with changed folios and running title in Introductory Note.

THE SAME. Cambridge: Printed at the Riverside Press. 1894 [1893].

8vo, pp. viii, 439. Vol. VIII of the Large-Paper Edition.

A limited edition of 150 copies printed from the same plates as the Riverside Edition and issued simultaneously.

TRANSLATION

WINTER. Gedanken und Stimmungsbilder. Deutsch von Emma Emmerich. München, 1900. Verlag Concord.

8vo, pp. 288.

ANTI–SLAVERY AND REFORM PAPERS

ANTI-SLAVERY | AND | REFORM PAPERS | By | Henry D. Thoreau | Selected and Edited | by H. S. Salt. | [*Device*] | London: | *Swan Sonnenschein & Co.,* | Paternoster Square. | 1890. | 12mo, pp. [iv], 141.

CONTENTS : —

Introductory Note [signed H. S. Salt].
Civil Disobedience.
A Plea for Captain John Brown.
The Last Days of John Brown.
Paradise (to be) Regained.
Life without Principle.

ESSAYS AND OTHER WRITINGS

ESSAYS AND OTHER WRITINGS | of Henry Thoreau: | Edited, with a Prefatory | Note, by Will H. Dircks. | London: | *Walter Scott*, 24 Warwick Lane, | Paternoster Row. [n. d.] [1891.] 16mo, pp. xvi, 271. In the Camelot series.

CONTENTS: —
Walking.
A Winter Walk.
Night and Moonlight.
The Landlord.
Life without Principle.
Civil Disobedience.
A Plea for Captain John Brown.
The Last Days of John Brown.
Love. (This and the next taken from a letter to Mr. Blake.)
Chastity and Sensuality.
Thomas Carlyle and his Works.
Letters. (A selection from *Letters to Various Persons*.)
Poems. (From *Letters to Various Persons*.)

AUTUMN

AUTUMN: From the Journal | of Henry D. Thoreau | Edited by H. G. O. Blake | [*Mottoes*] | [*Device*] | Boston and New York | *Houghton, Mifflin and Company* | The Riverside Press, Cambridge | 1892.

12mo, pp. vi, 470. Collation: i, title; ii, copyright and printer's imprint; iii–vi, Preface, signed The Editor; 1–459, text; 460, blank; 461–470, index.

AUTUMN | From the Journal of | Henry David
Thoreau | Edited by | H. G. O. Blake | [*Mottoes*] |
[*Device*] | Boston and New York | *Houghton,
Mifflin and Company* | The Riverside Press,
Cambridge | MDCCCXCIV [1893].

Crown 8vo, pp. vi, 470. Vol. VI of the Riverside Edition. With Preface (4 pp.), signed The
Editor, and index.

Printed from the plates of the first edition. The half-
title at the beginning is not included in the pagination.

THE SAME. Cambridge: Printed at the Riverside
Press. 1894 [1893].

8vo, pp. vi, 470. Vol. VII of the Large-Paper
Edition.

A limited edition of 150 copies issued simultaneously
with the Riverside Edition and printed from the same
plates.

MISCELLANIES

MISCELLANIES | By | Henry David Thoreau |
With a Biographical Sketch | by | Ralph Waldo
Emerson | and a General Index | to the Writ-
ings | [*Device*] | Boston and New York | *Hough-
ton, Mifflin and Company* | The Riverside
Press, Cambridge | MDCCCXCIV [1893].

Crown 8vo, pp. xii, 429. Vol. X of the Riverside Edition. With Introductory Note (5 pp.),
General Index (65 pp.), and steel engraving
of the Dunshee ambrotype of Thoreau. Collation: i, half-title; ii, blank; iii, title; iv, copyright and printer's imprint; v, contents; vi,
blank; vii–xi, Introductory Note; xii, blank;

1–33, Biographical Sketch; 34, blank; 35–364, text; 365–429, General Index.

CONTENTS : —

Biographical Sketch, pp. 1–33.

The Service: Qualities of the Recruit, pp. 35–37.
Now first collected. Reprinted from *Concord Lectures in Philosophy.*

Paradise (to be) Regained, pp. 38–69.

Herald of Freedom, pp. 70–75.

Wendell Phillips before the Concord Lyceum, pp. 76–80.

Thomas Carlyle and his Works, pp. 81–130.

Civil Disobedience, pp. 131–170.

Slavery in Massachusetts, pp. 171–196.

A Plea for Captain John Brown, pp. 197–236.

The Last Days of John Brown, pp. 237–248.

After the Death of John Brown, pp. 249–252.
Now first collected. Reprinted from *Echoes from Harper's Ferry.*

Life without Principle, pp. 253–287.

The Prometheus Bound of Æschylus, pp. 288–336.

Translations from Pindar, pp. 337–357.

Poems, pp. 358–364.
Inspiration (28 lines).
Pilgrims.
To a Stray Fowl.
The Black Knight.
The Moon.
Omnipresence.
Inspiration (quatrain).
Prayer.
Mission.
Delay.

The prose pieces except as otherwise indicated were reprinted from *A Yankee in Canada, with Anti-Slavery and Reform Papers.* The translations and four of the poems — "To a Stray Fowl," "The Black Knight," "The Moon," and "Prayer" — were reprinted from

The Dial. "Inspiration" (the longer poem of that name)
was reprinted from *Letters to Various Persons,* and the
four quatrains, "Omnipresence," "Inspiration," "Mission," and "Delay," had previously appeared in the *Critic*
for March 26, 1881. "Pilgrims" had been included by
George Parsons Lathrop in his volume entitled *A Masque
of Poets,* issued by Roberts Bros. in their No Name Series
in 1878, where it appeared anonymously.

FAMILIAR LETTERS

FAMILIAR LETTERS OF | HENRY DAVID THOREAU |
Edited, with an Introduction and Notes | by |
F. B. Sanborn | [*Device*] | Boston and New
York | *Houghton, Mifflin and Company* | The
Riverside Press, Cambridge | 1894.

Crown 8vo, pp. xii, 483. Uniform with
the Riverside Edition of Thoreau's Writings.
Frontispiece portrait reproduced in photogravure from the medallion by Walton Ricketson. Collation : i, title ; ii, copyright and printer's
imprint ; iii, contents ; iv, blank ; v–xii, Introduction, signed F. B. S., Concord, Mass.,
March 1, 1894 ; 1–464, text ; 465–483, index.

This book contains all the letters printed in *Letters to
Various Persons* and others besides, together with a connective tissue of biographical and explanatory matter.

THE SAME. Large-Paper Edition. 1894.

8vo, pp. xii, 483. Uniform with the Large-
Paper Edition of Thoreau's Writings. With
portrait reproduced in photogravure from the
Ricketson medallion.

Printed from the plates of the previous edition and
published four months earlier. Limited to 150 copies.

THE WRITINGS OF | HENRY DAVID THOREAU |
FAMILIAR LETTERS | Edited by F. B. Sanborn |
Enlarged Edition | [*Device*] | Boston and New
York | *Houghton Mifflin and Company* |
MDCCCCVI.

8vo, pp. xvi, 460. ·Vol. VI of the Manuscript
Edition, limited to 600 copies. With portrait,
five photogravure illustrations from photographs by Herbert W. Gleason, and a General
Index to the six volumes of Thoreau's Works,
including the Letters. Collation: i, half-title;
ii, number of set; iii, title; iv, copyright; v, vi,
contents; vii, list of illustrations; viii, blank;
ix–xv, Introduction signed F. B. S.; xvi, blank;
1, half-title; 2, blank; 3–400, text; 401, half-
title; 402, blank; 403–413, appendix; 414,
blank; 415, half-title; 416, numbered list of volumes included in the index; 417–460, General
Index; [461], blank; [462], printer's imprint.

The portrait is a photogravure of the Ricketson medallion. "The present volume is enlarged by some thirty
pages, chiefly by additional letters to Ricketson, and
all those to C. H. Greene" (Introduction). The Ricketson letters are incorporated in the text in their chronological places; the letters to Calvin H. Greene of
Rochester, Mich., and also two to Isaac Hecker, together with comment thereon, form the appendix. The
Introduction is dated Concord, Mass., March 1, 1906.
See also description of this edition on pp. 52, 53.

THE SAME. Boston and New York: *Houghton,
Mifflin & Co.* 1906.

12mo, pp. xvi, 460. Vol. VI of the Walden
Edition. With portrait, five photogravure illus-

trations from photographs by Herbert W. Gleason, and a General Index to the six volumes of
Thoreau's Works, including the Letters. Collation as in Manuscript Edition except that p. ii
is blank.

Printed from the plates of the Manuscript Edition and
having the same illustrations.

POEMS OF NATURE

POEMS OF NATURE | By Henry David Thoreau |
Selected and Edited by Henry S. Salt | and
Frank B. Sanborn | [*Device*] | Boston and New
York | *Houghton, Mifflin & Co.* | London:
John Lane | The Bodley Head | MDCCCXCV.

16mo, pp. xx, 122. Collation: i, ii, blank;
iii, half-title; iv, blank; v, title; vi, blank; vii–
ix, contents; x, blank; xi–xix, Introduction;
xx, blank; 1–122, text.

The Introduction says: " The fifty poems here brought
together . . . are perhaps two thirds of those which
Thoreau preserved. Many of them were printed by him,
in whole or in part, among his early contributions to
Emerson's *Dial*, or in his own two volumes, the *Week*
and *Walden*, which were all that were issued in his
lifetime. Others were given to Mr. Sanborn for publication, by Sophia Thoreau, the year after her brother's
death (several appeared in the *Boston Commonwealth*
in 1863); or have been furnished from time to time by
Mr. Blake, his literary executor."

CONTENTS: —

Nature.
    Hitherto unpublished.
Inspiration.
    Reprinted from the *Commonwealth*.

Sic Vita.

The Fisher's Boy.

The Atlantides.

The Aurora of Guido.

> Previously unpublished.

Sympathy.

Friendship.

True Kindness.

To the Maiden in the East.

> Five of the nine stanzas had appeared in the *Week*.

Free Love.

Rumors from an Æolian Harp.

Lines: "Though all the Fates should prove unkind."

Stanzas: "Away! away! away! away!"

A River Scene.

River Song.

Some Tumultuous Little Rill.

Boat Song.

To My Brother.

> Reprinted from Sanborn's *Thoreau*.

Stanzas: "Nature doth have her dawn each day."

The Inward Morning.

Greece.

> Reprinted from the *Commonwealth*. The last four of the twelve lines were used in the *Week*.

The Funeral Bell.

> Reprinted from the *Commonwealth*.

The Summer Rain.

Mist.

Smoke.

Haze.

The Moon.

The Vireo.

The Poet's Delay.

Lines: "All things are current found."

Nature's Child.

The Fall of the Leaf.

> All but the last three stanzas were first printed in the *Commonwealth*, a part of it under the title of ".The Soul's Season."

Winter Memories.

Stanzas written at Walden.

The Thaw.

> Previously unpublished, except that the first two lines appeared in *Excursions* in a slightly different form.

A Winter Scene.

> Previously unpublished.

The Crow.

To a Stray Fowl.

Mountains.

The Respectable Folks.

Poverty.

> Previously unpublished.

Conscience.

Pilgrims.

The Departure.

> Previously printed in the *Commonwealth* and Sanborn's *Thoreau*.

Independence.

> First printed in full in the *Commonwealth*. The last fourteen lines had appeared under the title of "The Black Knight" in *The Dial* and had been reprinted in *Miscellanies*.

Ding Dong.

> Previously unpublished. See p. 47.

My Prayer.

Except as otherwise noted, these poems had previously been published in the *Week*, *Walden*, *Excursions*, and *Miscellanies*, but very often without titles.

UNPUBLISHED LETTERS

Some Unpublished | Letters of | Henry D. and Sophia E. | Thoreau | A Chapter in the History | of a Still-born Book | [*Motto*] | Edited with a Prefatory Note | By | Samuel Arthur Jones | [*Device*] | Printed on the *Marion Press* | Jamaica, Queensborough, New York | 1899 [1898].

8vo, pp. xxxvi, 86.   Six heliotype illustrations.

One hundred and fifty copies printed. The letters by
Thoreau included are six addressed to Calvin H. Greene
of Rochester, Mich. They are reprinted in the Manuscript and Walden editions of the *Familiar Letters*.

OF FRIENDSHIP

OF FRIENDSHIP | An Essay from | A Week on
the Concord and | Merrimack Rivers | Henry
David Thoreau | [*Ornament*] | The Riverside
Press | 1901.

Tall 12mo, pp. vi, 88.

Five hundred numbered copies printed.

Here then is that Helpful as well | as Ennobling
Discourse entitled | THE ESSAY ON | FRIEND-
SHIP | by | Henry D. Thoreau. | Done into a
Book by the *Roycrofters* at | the Shop in East
Aurora, New York: MCMIII.

4to, pp. [iv], 36. With illuminated initials
and colophon.

The Friendship essay excerpted from the *Week*.

THE SERVICE

THE SERVICE | By Henry David Thoreau |
Edited by F. B. Sanborn | [*Device*] | Boston |
Charles E. Goodspeed | 1902.

Tall 8vo, pp. xii, 31.

Printed from an old manuscript of Thoreau's found in
Emerson's portfolios, bearing pencil date of July, 1840.
With notes by the editor. This is the complete form of the
essay, a part of which was included in *Miscellanies*. Most
of its contents will be found scattered through the earlier
pages of the *Journal*. A limited edition of 500 copies
printed.

LIFE WITHOUT PRINCIPLE

LIFE WITHOUT PRINCIPLE. With a short Biography of the Author by Ralph Waldo Emerson. A Reprint: Published for Subscribers at the *Sign of the Hop-Pole*, Eden Bridge, which is in Kent, England. 1902.

Tall 32mo, pp. 56.

One thousand copies printed.

THE SAME. London: *A. C. Fifield*. 1905. 12mo.

CIVIL DISOBEDIENCE

ON THE DUTY OF CIVIL DISOBEDIENCE. London: *The Simple Life Press*, 5 Water Lane, E. C. 1903.

18mo, pp. 38. With a note signed A. C. F. and a supplementary paper, entitled "The Cost of Disobedience," signed W. L. H.

FIRST AND LAST JOURNEYS

THE | FIRST AND LAST JOURNEYS | OF | THOREAU | Lately discovered among his unpublished journals | and manuscripts | Edited by | Franklin Benjamin Sanborn | [*Device*] | Boston: MDCDV | Printed exclusively for members of | *The Bibliophile Society*.

2 vols. 8vo, pp. xxxix, 146, 134. With portrait (from Dunshee ambrotype) and facsimiles of Thoreau's manuscripts. Prefatory Note signed H. H. H. Introduction by F. B. Sanborn. Addendum in vol. i; index in vol. ii.

A considerable part of the first volume appears in substantially the same form in the *Week* and the *Journal*. This book was not actually distributed till 1907. The " first journey " is the one on the Concord and Merrimac Rivers described in the *Week ;* the "last" is the trip to Minnesota with young Horace Mann in 1861. There are also fragments of the Staten Island journal of 1843 and a part of an essay on Conversation. The Addendum to vol. i consists of various fragments of journals and other writings, including a number of poems not otherwise published. The manuscripts, consisting of fragments of Thoreau's original journals, drafts of essays, and rough pencil notes, are the property of Mr. W. K. Bixby of St. Louis.

Following is a list of the verse contained in vol. i:—

Morning: "Thou unconverted Saint," p. xiv.
> Another form of the bit of verse beginning "An early unconverted Saint " printed in the *Week*, containing four additional lines.

"Upon the bank at early dawn," pp. xvi, xvii.
> Nine four-line stanzas.

The Breeze's Invitation: "Like two careless swifts let's sail," p. 51.
> Four five-line stanzas. The complete poem in six stanzas appears in *Journal*, vol. i, p. 86.

Epitaph on Pursy: "Traveller, this is no prison," pp. 81, 82.
> A part was used in the *Week* in somewhat altered form in the lines beginning " Here lies an honest man."

Epitaph on the World: "Here lies the body of this world," p. 82.

"Heathen without reproach," p. 122.
> Eight lines. Another form of " Morning," cited above.

To the Mountains: "And when the sun puts out his lamp," p. 123.
> Twenty-two lines.

Fog: "Dull water-spirit and Protean god," p. 126.
> Ten lines. Another form of the poem beginning "Low-anchored cloud" used in the *Week*.

The Friend: "The great Friend," pp. 126–128.
> Forty lines.

The Battle of Life: "How little curious is man," p. 129.

Twenty-six lines. This poem with two additional lines appears in *Journal*, vol. i, pp. 459, 460.

The Threadbare Trees: "The threadbare trees so poor and thin," p. 130.

Three four-line stanzas. The third stanza was used in the poem "Inspiration."

"Until at length the north winds blow," p. 132.

Four lines.

The Virgin: "With her calm, inquiring eyes," p. 134.

Eight lines.

Solitude: "We walk in Nature still alone," pp. 134, 135.

Thirty-two lines. This appears in somewhat different form as the latter part of the poem "To a Marsh Hawk in Spring," in *Journal*, vol. i, pp. 472, 473.

"Love equals swift and slow," p. 136.

Four lines. Printed in the first edition of the *Week*, p. 285.

True Freedom: "Wait not till slaves pronounce the word," pp. 137, 138.

Eleven four-line stanzas.

Our Neighbors: "The respectable folks," pp. 139, 140.

Twenty-five lines. Another form of the poem in the *Week*.

"My ground is high," p. 140.

Four lines. The same with four additional lines appears in *Journal*, vol. i, p. 245.

"If from your price ye will not swerve," pp. 140, 141.

Ten lines. This appears in *Journal*, vol. i, pp. 245, 246.

Independence: "Ye princes, keep your realms," p. 141.

Four four-line stanzas. A different form of the poem of this title printed in the *Commonwealth* and in *Poems of Nature* and *Excursions, and Poems*.

A Winter and Spring Scene: "The willows droop," pp. 144–146.

Eighty-two lines. A longer and otherwise different form of "A Winter Scene" as published in *Poems of Nature*, p. 90.

SIR WALTER RALEIGH

SIR WALTER RALEIGH | By | Henry David Thoreau | Lately discovered among his unpublished journals | and manuscripts | Introduction by | Franklin Benjamin Sanborn | Edited

by | Henry Aiken Metcalf | [*Device*] | Boston:
MDCDV | Printed exclusively for members
of |*The Bibliophile Society.*

8vo, pp. xiv, 106. With portrait of Raleigh.
Preface signed Henry Aiken Metcalf. Introduction and Notes by F. B. Sanborn.

Written, the Introduction states, between 1842 and
1845, probably for *The Dial.* (See, however, pp. 115, 116.)
Though bearing the date 1905, the book was not actually
distributed till 1907. This essay appears in small part
in the *Week* and in the first volume of the *Journal.* The
manuscript is owned by Mr. W. K. Bixby of St. Louis.

CAPE COD, AND MISCELLANIES

THE WRITINGS OF | HENRY DAVID THOREAU |
CAPE COD | AND | MISCELLANIES | [*Device*] |
Boston and New York | *Houghton Mifflin
and Company* | MDCCCCVI.

8vo, pp. xii, 489. Vol. IV of the Manuscript
Edition, limited to 600 copies. With Introductory Note and five photogravure illustrations from photographs by Herbert W. Gleason.
Collation: i, half-title; ii, number of set; iii,
title; iv, copyright; v, vi, contents; vii, list of
illustrations; viii, blank; ix–xii, Introductory
Note; 1, half-title; 2, blank; 3–273, Cape Cod;
274, blank; 275, half-title; 276, blank; 277–
482, Miscellanies; 483, half-title; 484, blank;
485–489, index; [490], printer's imprint.

The contents of the Miscellanies are identical with
those of the Riverside *Miscellanies*, except that the
Biographical Sketch and the Poems are omitted. See
also description of this edition on pp. 52, 53.

THE SAME. Boston and New York: *Houghton, Mifflin & Co.* 1906.

12mo, pp. xii, 489. Vol. IV of the Walden Edition. With Introductory Note and five photogravure illustrations from photographs by Herbert W. Gleason. Collation as in Manuscript Edition except that p. ii is blank.

Printed from the plates of the Manuscript Edition and having the same illustrations.

EXCURSIONS, AND POEMS

THE WRITINGS OF | HENRY DAVID THOREAU | EXCURSIONS | AND | POEMS | [*Device*] | Boston and New York | *Houghton Mifflin and Company* | MDCCCCVI.

8vo, pp. xvi, 431. Vol. V of the Manuscript Edition, limited to 600 copies. With Introductory Note and five photogravure illustrations from photographs by Herbert W. Gleason. Collation: i, half-title; ii, number of set; iii, title; iv, copyright; v–vii, contents; viii, blank; ix, list of illustrations; x, blank; xi–xv, Introductory Note; xvi, blank; 1, half-title; 2, mottoes; 3–333, Excursions; 334, blank; 335, half-title; 336, blank; 337–392, Translations; 393, half-title; 394, blank; 395–419, Poems; 420–422, A List of the Poems and Bits of Verse scattered among Thoreau's Prose Writings exclusive of the Journal; 423, half-title; 424, blank; 425–431, index; [432], printers' imprint.

The *Excursions* are identical with those of the Riverside Edition, except that "May Days" and "Days and Nights in Concord" are "omitted as consisting merely of extracts from Thoreau's Journal and therefore superseded by the publication of the latter in its complete form." The collection of Poems (and Translations) is based on that in the Riverside *Miscellanies* and on *Poems of Nature*. Poems occurring in other volumes of the Manuscript Edition are omitted and no unpublished or uncollected pieces are added. See also description of this edition on pp. 52, 53.

CONTENTS OF TRANSLATIONS AND POEMS: —

TRANSLATIONS.

The Prometheus Bound of Æschylus.
Translations from Pindar.

POEMS.

Nature.
Inspiration.
The Aurora of Guido.
To the Maiden in the East.
To my Brother.
Greece.
The Funeral Bell.
The Moon.
The Fall of the Leaf.
The Thaw.
A Winter Scene.
To a Stray Fowl.
Poverty.
Pilgrims.
The Departure.
Independence.
Ding Dong.
Omnipresence.
Inspiration (quatrain).
Mission.
Delay.
Prayer.

THE SAME. Boston and New York: *Houghton, Mifflin & Co.* 1906.

12mo, pp. xvi, 431. Vol. v of the Walden Edition. With Introductory Note and five photogravure illustrations from photographs by Herbert W. Gleason. Collation as in Manuscript Edition except that p. ii is blank.

Printed from the plates of the Manuscript Edition and having the same illustrations.

JOURNAL

THE WRITINGS OF | HENRY DAVID THOREAU | JOURNAL | Edited by Bradford Torrey | I [II–XIV] | 1837–1846 [other dates in other volumes]. [*Device*, red] | Boston and New York | *Houghton Mifflin and Company* | MDCCCCVI.

8vo, pp. lii, 488; (II) xii, 505; (III) xii, 487; (IV) xii, 495; (V) xii, 532; (VI) x, 491; (VII) xii, 527; (VIII) x, 468; (IX) xii, 503; (X) xii, 511; (XI) xii, 457; (XII) xii, 458; (XIII) x, 430; (XIV) x, 459. Vols. VII–XX of the Manuscript Edition. Collation of Vol. I: i, half-title "The Writings of Henry David Thoreau, in twenty volumes, volume VII;" ii, "Manuscript Edition, limited to six hundred copies, Number [ ];" iii, title; iv, copyright; v, vi, Publishers' Note; vii–ix, Editor's Preface; x, blank; xi–xv, contents; xvi, blank; xvii, list of illustrations; xviii, blank; xix–li, Introduction, signed B. T.; lii, blank; 1, half-title, "Henry D. Thoreau, Gleanings, or What Time has not reaped of my Journal;" 2, explanatory matter and poetical mottoes; 3–488, text; [489], blank; [490], printers' imprint "The Riverside Press, H. O. Houghton and Company, Cambridge, Massachusetts." Vol. XIV contains (pp. 347–459) an index to the whole Journal.

This edition is illustrated with photogravures from photographs by Herbert W. Gleason and with cuts in the text from rude drawings by Thoreau. The frontispiece to vol. I is a photogravure from the Rowse crayon. Vol. XIV contains at the end, just before the index, an indexed map of Concord compiled by Herbert W. Gleason, showing the localities mentioned by Thoreau in his Journal. Further particulars as to the format will be found in the description of the Manuscript Edition of Thoreau's Writings, pp. 52, 53.

Extracts from the Journal had previously been published under the titles *Early Spring in Massachusetts*, *Summer*, *Winter*, and *Autumn*, and also in Channing's *Thoreau, the Poet-Naturalist* (q. v., pp. 81, 82) and in *Excursions*, Riverside Edition. Selections from the present complete *Journal*, also, were printed in the *Atlantic* in January–May, 1905, in advance of book publication.

Thoreau's Journal in thirty-nine manuscript volumes was bequeathed by his sister Sophia to Mr. H. G. O. Blake, who, upon his death, left it in turn to Mr. E. Harlow Russell of Worcester. Mr. Russell arranged with the publishers to bring it out *in extenso*. The greatest care was taken to produce an accurate text, and the work of copying, comparing, and printing the Journal occupied three years and a half. As printed it is virtually complete and unabridged, the few omissions noted in the Editor's Preface being of an unimportant character. The earliest volumes of the original Journal were destroyed by Thoreau in writing the *Week* and *Walden*, but transcripts of unused passages were taken and preserved. This explains the half-title preceding text quoted in collation above. The manuscript Journal after the printing was sold by Mr. Russell and is now in the possession of Mr. Stephen H. Wakeman of New York.

The dates covered by the several volumes are: —
   I. 1837–1846.
   II. 1850–September 15, 1851.
   III. September 16, 1851–April 30, 1852.
   IV. May 1, 1852–February 27, 1853.
   V. March 5–November 30, 1853.
   VI. December 1, 1853–August 31, 1854.
   VII. September 1, 1854–October 30, 1855.
   VIII. November 1, 1855–August 15, 1856.
   IX. August 16, 1856–August 7, 1857.
   X. August 8, 1857–June 29, 1858.
   XI. July 2, 1858–February 28, 1859.
   XII. March 2, 1859–November 30, 1859.
   XIII. December 1, 1859–July 31, 1860.
   XIV. August 1, 1860–November 3, 1861.

Following is a list of the verse contained in the *Journal* : —
VOL. I.
Friendship, p. 40: "I think awhile of Love, and, while I think."
The Bluebirds, p. 43.
May Morning, p. 49.
Walden, p. 50: "True, our converse a stranger is to speech."
"Truth, Goodness, Beauty, — those celestial thrins," p. 51.
"In the busy streets, domains of trade," p. 51.
Cliffs, p. 51: "The loudest sound that burdens here the breeze."
My Boots, p. 60.
Fair Haven, p. 62: "When winter fringes every bough."
   All but the last stanza, somewhat revised and without title, was printed in *Excursions*.
Anacreon's Ode to the Cicada, p. 66.
   Printed in *Excursions* with a single verbal variation.
Anacreontics.
   Return of Spring, p. 69.
     Printed in *Excursions*.
   Cupid Wounded, p. 70.
     Printed in the *Week* with variations in lines 2 and 3.

The Thaw, p. 71.

Has one more stanza than as printed in *Poems of Nature*.
"Last night, as I lay gazing with shut eyes," p. 71.

Love, p. 72: "We two that planets erst had been."

"The deeds of king and meanest hedger," p. 72.

" 'T will soon appear if we but look," p. 72.

The Evening Wind, p. 72: "The eastern mail comes lumbering in."

Printed in the *Week*.

The Peal of the Bells, p. 73.

Published in *Poems of Nature* under the title of "Ding Dong," somewhat revised and without the last stanza.

The Shrike, p. 74.

The second of the two stanzas was printed in *Excursions*.

Sympathy, p. 80: "Lately, alas, I knew a gentle boy."

Used in the *Week*. First printed in *The Dial*, July, 1840.

The "Book of Gems," p. 82.

The Assabet, p. 84: "Up this pleasant stream let's row."

Three or four of the twelve stanzas were printed in the *Week*.

The Breeze's Invitation, p. 86.

"Nature doth have her dawn each day," p. 87.

Printed in the *Week*. First printed in *The Dial*, January, 1841.

Farewell, p. 95.

Noon, p. 96.

"Each more melodious note I hear," p. 102.

Included in *The Service*.

The Fisher's Son, p. 110.

Of the nineteen stanzas, four, beginning "My years are like a stroll upon the beach," were used in the *Week* and four others were printed in the Introduction to the *Familiar Letters*.

"By a strong liking we prevail," p. 113.

The Freshet, p. 122.

The greater part of the poem, beginning with "The river swelleth more and more," appears in *Excursions*.

"Two years and twenty now have flown," p. 127.

Three of the five stanzas were used in the *Week* under the title of "The Poet's Delay."

"Wait not till I invite thee, but observe," p. 205.

Friendship, p. 242: "Now we are partners in such legal trade."

On the Sun coming out in the Afternoon, p. 243.

"They who prepare my evening meal below," p. 243.

"My ground is high," p. 245.

"If from your price ye will not swerve," p. 245.

Friendship's Steadfastness, p. 248.

"Death cannot come too soon," p. 249.

Wachusett, p. 256.

> A part of the poem "Mountains," beginning "With frontier strength ye stand your ground," printed in the *Week* and (abridged) in *Excursions*.

Westward, Ho! p. 259: "The needles of the pine."

> Printed in *Excursions*.

The Echo of the Sabbath Bell heard in the Woods, p. 259.

> Used in the *Week* with some variations and without title.

"My life hath been the poem I would have writ," p. 275.

> Used in the *Week* with a slight verbal variation.

"Greater is the depth of sadness," p. 283.

"Where I have been," p. 285.

"Better wait," p. 287.

"Packed in my mind lie all the clothes," p. 291.

> This, with the lines beginning on the succeeding page, was printed under the title of "The Inward Morning" in *The Dial* for October, 1842, and in the *Week*. This version contains an additional stanza (the second) and other variations.

"What is it gilds the trees and clouds," p. 292.

"Within the circuit of this plodding life," p. 304.

> Printed in revised form in *Excursions*.

"Tell me, ye wise ones, if ye can," p. 373.

> Eight lines of this poem, beginning "A finer race and finer fed," somewhat altered, were used in the *Week*.

"And Memnon's mother sprightly greets us now," p. 376.

> Six of the eight lines were used (with revision) in the *Week* in the stanza beginning "This is my Carnac, whose unmeasured dome."

"The Earth," p. 390.

The Hero, p. 403.

> Twenty-six lines of this, somewhat revised, appeared in *A Masque of Poets* (1878) under the title of "Pilgrims," and were reprinted in *Miscellanies*.

"At midnight's hour I raised my head," p. 407.

"I seek the present time," p. 409.

"I was born upon thy bank, river," p. 438.

"My friends, why should we live?" p. 447.

"I mark the summer's swift decline," p. 449.

"Far o'er the bow," p. 457.

The first four lines of a poem the remainder of which, beginning "Where gleaming fields of haze," was used in the *Week*.

"Methinks that by a strict behavior," p. 457.

"I have rolled near some other spirit's path," p. 457.

Fog, p. 457: "Thou drifting meadow of the air."

Used in the *Week* abridged and revised, beginning "Low-anchored cloud."

"How little curious is man," p. 459.

"On fields o'er which the reaper's hand has passed," p. 463.

To a Marsh Hawk in Spring, p. 471.

"I fain would stretch me by the highway-side," p. 477.

Another form of "The Thaw."

"Yet let us thank the purblind race," p. 477.

"I've seen ye, sisters, on the mountain-side," p. 477.

"Ye do commend me to all virtue ever," p. 479.

Vol. ii.

"And once again," p. 54.

"The man of wild habits," p. 54.

This and the preceding are parts of a poem printed in *Excursions* under the title of "The Old Marlborough Road," with considerable revision.

"Without inlet it lies," p. 57.

Two lines of this appear in *Walden* with other lines beginning "It is no dream of mine."

Tall Ambrosia, p. 59.

"I saw a delicate flower had grown up two feet high," p. 66.

"To-day I climbed a handsome rounded hill," p. 67.

"I am the little Irish boy," p. 117.

Vol. iii.

"I do not fear my thoughts will die," p. 113.

"I am the little Irish boy," p. 243.

Another form (see three lines above).

Vol. x.

"'T was thirty years ago," p. 138.
"Forever in my dream and in my morning thought," p. 144.
"The chickadee," p. 172.

The Writings of | Henry David Thoreau |
   Journal | Edited by Bradford Torrey | I
   [II–XIV] | [Journal dates] | [*Device*] | Boston
   and New York | *Houghton Mifflin and Com-
   pany* | The Riverside Press, Cambridge | 1906.
   12mo, pp. as in Manuscript Edition. Vols.
vii–xx of the Walden Edition. Collation of
Vol. i: i, half-title, "Walden Edition, The Writings of Henry David Thoreau;" ii, blank;
otherwise as in Manuscript Edition.

Printed from the plates of the Manuscript Edition
and having the same illustrations.

The *Journal* is as yet published only as a part of these
two editions of Thoreau's complete writings and is not
to be had separately.

GODFREY OF BOULOGNE

Unpublished Poems by Bryant and Thoreau :
   "Musings," by William Cullen Bryant, and
   "Godfrey of Boulogne," by Henry D.
   Thoreau. Boston: *Bibliophile Society*. 1907.
   8vo, pp. xxviii. Pages xxi, xxii, facsimile of
Thoreau's poem; xxiii, xxiv, Introduction by
F. B. Sanborn; xxvii, xxviii, the poem. Edition
limited to 470 copies printed for members of the
society.

COLLECTED WORKS

RIVERSIDE EDITION.

10 vols., crown 8vo. With portraits and Introductory Notes. Boston: *Houghton, Mifflin & Co.* 1894 [1893].

VOL. I. A WEEK ON THE CONCORD AND MERRIMACK RIVERS.

VOL. II. WALDEN; OR, LIFE IN THE WOODS.

VOL. III. THE MAINE WOODS.

VOL. IV. CAPE COD.

VOL. V. EARLY SPRING IN MASSACHUSETTS.

VOL. VI. SUMMER.

VOL. VII. AUTUMN.

VOL. VIII. WINTER.

VOL. IX. EXCURSIONS.

VOL. X. MISCELLANIES.

The portraits are from the Rowse crayon, the Worcester daguerreotype, and the New Bedford ambrotype. The Introductory Notes are biographical and bibliographical in character, and were prepared by Mr. Horace E. Scudder. Volume x has a General Index to the Writings. This was the first regularly collected complete edition of Thoreau's writings, but for some years before its publication Thoreau's books had been issued in a uniform 12mo style bound in green cloth with gilt tops. *Early Spring, Summer, Winter,* and *Autumn* made their first appearance in this 12mo form.

The *Familiar Letters,* upon its appearance in 1894, was added to the Riverside Edition as an eleventh volume, being brought out in uniform style, though it lacked the half-title with the volume-number.

LARGE–PAPER EDITION.

10 vols., 8vo. Cambridge: Printed at the Riverside Press. 1894 [1893].

Printed from the plates of the Riverside Edition and issued simultaneously with it. Limited to 150 numbered copies. The *Familiar Letters*, published in 1894, was first issued in a Large-Paper Edition uniform with this edition of Thoreau's writings.

MANUSCRIPT EDITION.

20 vols., 8vo. With 3 portraits and 101 illustrations from photographs by Herbert W. Gleason. Boston: *Houghton, Mifflin & Co.* 1906.

VOL. I. A WEEK ON THE CONCORD AND MERRIMACK RIVERS.

VOL. II. WALDEN.

VOL. III. THE MAINE WOODS.

VOL. IV. CAPE COD, AND MISCELLANIES.

VOL. V. EXCURSIONS, AND POEMS.

VOL. VI. FAMILIAR LETTERS. Edited by F. B. Sanborn.

VOLS. VII–XX. JOURNAL. Edited by Bradford Torrey.

This edition is based on the Riverside Edition, with the addition of the complete *Journal* in fourteen volumes. (See pp. 44–50, *Journal*.) Besides the changes in arrangement indicated by the volume-titles given above, it is to be noted that the Biographical Sketch by Emerson is transferred from *Excursions* to the first volume; a General Index to the "Works," the first six volumes of the set, is added to Vol. VI; and the four volumes of Journal extracts edited by Mr. H. G. O. Blake — *Early Spring in Massachusetts, Summer, Autumn,* and *Winter* — are omitted as having been superseded by the publication of the complete Journal. The two papers entitled "May Days" and "Days and Nights in Concord," consisting of extracts from Thoreau's Journal, which are printed in the Riverside Edition of *Excursions*, are omitted; the collection of Poems is enlarged by the addition of a number of poems taken from *Poems of Nature;* and the *Familiar Letters* is revised and enlarged by the editor.

The fourteen volumes of the *Journal* contain many text cuts from rude sketches by Thoreau. The last volume has a "Map of Concord, Mass., showing Localities mentioned by Thoreau in his Journals, compiled by Herbert W. Gleason, 1906," with a two-page index to the same.

This edition was limited to six hundred numbered copies, and the first volume of each set contains a piece of Thoreau's autograph manuscript mounted and bound in before the frontispiece. These manuscripts vary in interest, some of them adding materially to the value of the sets. Some of the sets, issued in fine bindings, have two frontispieces to each volume, a carbon photograph of a flower and a colored photogravure. The edition was printed on a specially manufactured paper with "Thoreau" in the watermark.

WALDEN EDITION.

20 vols., 12mo. Boston: *Houghton, Mifflin & Co.* 1906.

Printed from the same plates as the Manuscript Edition, which it followed. Sold only by subscription for the entire set.

SELECTIONS FROM THOREAU'S
WRITINGS

SELECTIONS FROM THOREAU'S WRITINGS

BOOKS ENTIRELY DEVOTED TO THOREAU

THE SUCCESSION OF FOREST TREES, WILD APPLES, AND SOUNDS. With a Biographical Sketch by Ralph Waldo Emerson. Boston: *Houghton, Mifflin & Co.* [1887.]

16mo, paper, pp. 103. No. 27 of the Riverside Literature Series. With a Preface and annotations for the use of schools.

THOREAU'S THOUGHTS | Selections from the Writings | of Henry David Thoreau | Edited by | H. G. O. Blake | [*Motto*] | [*Device*] | Boston and New York | *Houghton, Mifflin and Company* | The Riverside Press, Cambridge | 1890.

16mo, pp. vi, 153. Collation: i, title; ii, copyright; iii–v, Introductory; vi, blank; 1–123, Selections from Thoreau; 124, blank; 125, half-title with motto; 126, blank; 127–129, Preface; 130, blank; 131–146, A Contribution toward a Bibliography of Henry David Thoreau [by Dr. Samuel A. Jones]; 147–153, index.

SELECTIONS FROM | THOREAU | Edited, with an Introduction | by | Henry S. Salt | Author of 'The Life of Henry David Thoreau' | London | *Macmillan and Co.* | 1895 | All rights reserved.

16mo, pp. xxii, 330. Photogravure portrait.

From *A Week on the Concord and Merrimack Rivers*.
 Concord River, pp. 1–12.
 Sunday Thoughts, pp. 13–28.
 Friendship, pp. 29–41.
From *Walden*.
 Where I Lived and What I Lived for, pp. 42–63.
 Higher Laws, pp. 64–79.
 House-Warming, pp. 80–88.
From *The Maine Woods*.
 Primeval Nature, pp. 89–102.
 The Murder of the Moose, pp. 103–117.
 Forest Phenomena, pp. 118–123.
From *Cape Cod*.
 The Shipwreck, pp. 124–135.
 The Beach, pp. 136–150.
 The Wellfleet Oysterman, pp. 151–167.
From *Excursions*.
 Natural History of Massachusetts, pp. 168–198.
 Walking, pp. 199–237.
From *Anti-Slavery and Reform Papers*.
 Civil Disobedience, pp. 238–266.
 A Plea for Captain John Brown, pp. 267–300.
 Life without Principle, pp. 301–330.

EXTRACTS FROM THOREAU. Selected by Emily
 R. Lyman. [*Mottoes.*] Philadelphia: Printed
 by *J. B. Lippincott Co.* MDCCCXCIX.
  Crown 8vo, pp. 175. Ten illustrations from
 photographs.
  A limited number printed for private distribution only
 Preface signed E. R. L.

LIFE AND FRIENDSHIP. Selected from Essays and
 Diaries of Henry D. Thoreau. Prefatory Note
 by Harry Roberts. London: *Anthony Treherne
 & Co.* 1904.
  18mo, pp. 218.

HENRY D. THOREAU: A LITTLE BOOK OF NATURE
THEMES. Selected by Thomas Coke Watkins.
Portland, Me.: *Thomas B. Mosher*. 1906 [1907].
32mo, pp. xvi, 80. With a Foreword.

Selections from the *Week* and *Walden*, with one of
Channing's composite quotations from Thoreau's Journal
printed as a "Proem."

GOLDEN THOUGHTS FROM THOREAU. Edited
with a Preface by Dorothy Eastwood. London:
John Lane. [1907.]
18mo, pp. xvi, 115.

Short selections classified under the heads of Man,
Solitude and Society, etc., together with two of the
poems.

IN TOUCH WITH THOREAU. Quotations from
the Writings of Henry D. Thoreau. Compiled
by Harriet A. Townsend. Buffalo. 1907.
Privately printed.

A year-book, with a Foreword in verse signed H. A. T.

A HAPPY LIFE: THOUGHTS FROM THOREAU.
London: *C. W. Daniel*. 1907.
16mo.

Listed in the English Catalogue.

OTHER BOOKS CONTAINING SELECTIONS
FROM THOREAU

CYCLOPÆDIA OF AMERICAN LITERATURE. Edited
by Evert A. Duyckinck and George L. Duyckinck. New York: *Charles Scribner*. 1855.

Extracts from *Walden*, Vol. II, pp. 654–656.

A HANDBOOK OF ENGLISH LITERATURE. AMERI-
CAN AUTHORS. By Francis H. Underwood.
Boston: *Lee & Shepard.* 1872.

Three short selections from *Walden*, pp. 415–417. The
running-title of the book is "Handbook of American
Authors."

PARNASSUS. Edited by Ralph Waldo Emerson.
Boston: *James R. Osgood & Co.* 1874.

Smoke, p. 47.
Mist, p. 48.
Haze, p. 48.
Sympathy, pp. 78, 79.
Inspiration, pp. 94, 95.

APPLETON'S FIFTH READER. By William T.
Harris, Andrew J. Rickoff, Mark Bailey.
New York: *D. Appleton & Co.* [1879.]

Five selections from Thoreau, with notes.
The Battle of the Ants (from *Walden*), pp. 27–31.
Ascent of Mount Ktaadn (from *The Maine Woods*),
pp. 121–127.
In the Maine Woods, pp. 165–168.
Building the House (from *Walden*), pp. 224–227.
Walden Pond (from *Walden*), pp. 228–231.

McGUFFEY'S FIFTH ECLECTIC READER. Cincin-
nati: *Van Antwerp, Bragg & Co.* [1879.]

Transportation and Planting of Seed (from *Excursions*),
pp. 278–282.

AMERICAN PROSE. Edited by Horace E. Scudder.
Boston: *Houghton, Osgood & Co.* 1880.

Sounds (from *Walden*), pp. 302–323.
Brute Neighbors (from *Walden*), pp. 323–337.
The Highland Light (from *Cape Cod*), pp. 338–365.

THE SAME. Revised and Enlarged Edition. Boston: *Houghton, Mifflin & Co.* 1891.

> Sounds, pp. 311–329.
> Brute Neighbors, pp. 329–342.
> The Highland Light, pp. 342–366.

LITTLE CLASSICS: NATURE. Edited by Rossiter Johnson. Boston: *Houghton, Mifflin & Co.* 1880.

> A Winter Walk, pp. 91–111.

HARPER'S CYCLOPÆDIA OF BRITISH AND AMERICAN POETRY. Edited by Epes Sargent. New York: *Harper & Bros.* 1881.

> Smoke in Winter, p. 745.
> Upon the Beach ("My life is like a stroll upon the Beach"), pp. 745, 746.

HALF-HOURS WITH THE BEST AMERICAN AUTHORS. Edited by Charles Morris. Philadelphia: *J. B. Lippincott Co.* [1886.]

> Ascending Ktaadn, pp. 39–47.

A LIBRARY OF AMERICAN LITERATURE. Edited by Edmund Clarence Stedman and Ellen Mackay Hutchinson. New York: *Charles L. Webster & Co.* 1889.

> Spring beside Walden (from *Walden*), vol. vii, pp. 323–327.
> The Fisher's Boy (the four stanzas from *Letters to Various Persons*), vol. vii, p. 327.
> Mist, vol. vii, p. 328.
> The Wellfleet Oysterman (from *Cape Cod*), vol. vii, pp. 328–336.

MASTERPIECES OF AMERICAN LITERATURE. Boston: *Houghton, Mifflin & Co.* 1891.

> Wild Apples, pp. 166–197.

A NEW LIBRARY OF POETRY AND SONG. Edited by William Cullen Bryant. Revised and Enlarged Edition. New York: *Fords, Howard & Hulbert.* 1895.

> Smoke, p. 691.
> Mist, p. 691.

THE LIBRARY OF CHOICE LITERATURE AND ENCYCLOPÆDIA OF UNIVERSAL AUTHORSHIP. Edited by Ainsworth R. Spofford and Charles Gibbon. Philadelphia: *The Gebbie Publishing Co.* 1895.

> My House (from *Walden*), vol. vi, pp. 220–222.

NATURE'S DIARY. Compiled by Francis H. Allen. Boston: *Houghton, Mifflin & Co.* 1897.

> Contains many extracts from Thoreau's writings.

LIBRARY OF THE WORLD'S BEST LITERATURE. Edited by Charles Dudley Warner. New York: *R. S. Peale & J. A. Hill.* 1897.

> Inspiration, pp. 14877–14879.
> The Fisher's Boy, p. 14879.
> Smoke, p. 14880.
> Work and Pay (from *Walden*), pp. 14880–14883.
> Solitude (from *Walden*), pp. 14884–14891.
> The Bean Field (from *Walden*), pp. 14891–14897.
> Walking (from *Excursions*), pp. 14897–14908.

AMERICAN PROSE. Edited by George Rice Carpenter. New York: *The Macmillan Co.* 1898.

> Style in Writing, pp. 343–345.
> A Village Festival, pp. 346–348.
> Personal Aims, pp. 348–351.
> Sounds at Evening, pp. 351–353.
> Solitude, pp. 353–355.
> Immortality, pp. 356, 357.

THE INTERNATIONAL LIBRARY OF FAMOUS LITERATURE. Edited by Donald G. Mitchell and Andrew Lang. New York: *Merrill & Baker*. 1898.

> Walden Pond in Winter (from *Walden*), pp. 5172–5183.

AN AMERICAN ANTHOLOGY. Edited by Edmund Clarence Stedman. Boston: *Houghton, Mifflin & Co.* 1900.

> Inspiration, p. 182.
> The Fisher's Boy, pp. 182, 183.
> Smoke, p. 183.
> Mist, p. 183.

THE LIBRARY OF LITERARY CRITICISM OF ENGLISH AND AMERICAN AUTHORS. Edited by Charles Wells Moulton. Buffalo: *The Moulton Publishing Co.* 1901.

> Short selections on the following authors: Shakespeare, vol. i, p. 561; Quarles, vol. ii, p. 78; Hawthorne, vol. vi, p. 342; Carlyle, vol. vii, p. 261; Alcott, vol. vii, p. 662.

THE POETS OF TRANSCENDENTALISM. Edited by George Willis Cooke. Boston: *Houghton, Mifflin & Co.* 1903.

> Stanzas: "Nature doth have her dawn each day," p. 62.
> Inspiration, p. 63.
> My Prayer, p. 67.
> Rumors from an Æolian Harp, p. 68.
> Conscience, p. 69.
> The Inward Morning, p. 71.
> Lines: "All things are current found," p. 73.
> My Life: "My life is like a stroll upon the beach," p. 74.

CHAMBERS'S CYCLOPÆDIA OF ENGLISH LITERATURE. New Edition by David Patrick. Philadelphia: *J. B. Lippincott Co.* 1904 [1903].

Building the Chimney (from *Walden*), pp. 794, 795.
What he Lived for (from *Walden*), p. 795.
Rumours from an Æolian Harp, p. 795.
Haze, p. 795.
My Prayer, p. 796.
Nature ("O Nature, I do not aspire"), p. 796.
The Fisher's Boy (four stanzas), p. 796.

MODERN ENGLISH PROSE. Selected and Edited by George Rice Carpenter and William Tenney Brewster. New York: *The Macmillan Co.* 1904.

Where I Lived, and what I Lived for (from *Walden*), pp. 370–384.

IN PRAISE OF WALKING. THOREAU, WHITMAN, BURROUGHS, HAZLITT. London: *A. C. Fifield.* 1905.

Listed in the English Catalogue. The compiler has not seen a copy of it.

WALKING: A FINE ART. Compiled and Edited by Edward F. Bigelow. Salem, Mass.: *Samuel E. Cassino & Son.* [1907.]

Extracts from "Walking" in *Excursions*, and from *Summer*, *Winter*, and *Autumn*, pp. 61–75.

ARTICLES AND POEMS BY THOREAU

THOREAU'S ARTICLES AND POEMS ARRANGED CHRONOLOGICALLY BY MEDIA OF PUBLICATION

THE DIAL.

VOL. I, No. 1, July, 1840.

SYMPATHY, "Lately alas, I knew a gentle boy," p. 71. Signed T.

Reprinted in *A Week on the Concord and Merrimack Rivers*, first edition, p. 274; second edition, p. 276; Riverside Edition, p. 343; Walden Edition,[1] p. 276; in *Letters to Various Persons,* p. 211; and in *Poems of Nature,* p. 21.

AULUS PERSIUS FLACCUS, p. 117. Signed T.

Reprinted in *A Week on the Concord and Merrimack Rivers*, first edition, p. 324; second edition, p. 326; Riverside Edition, p. 405; Walden Edition, p. 327.

VOL. I, No. 3, Jan., 1841.

STANZAS, "Nature doth have her dawn each day," p. 314. Signed D. H. T.

Reprinted in *Week*, first edition, p. 298; second edition, p. 301; Riverside Edition, p. 375; Walden Edition, p. 302; and in *Poems of Nature*, p. 56.

VOL. II, No. 1, July, 1841.

SIC VITA, "I am a parcel of vain strivings tied," p. 81. Signed H. D. T.

Reprinted in *Week*, first edition, p. 403; second edition, p. 405; Riverside Edition, p. 506; Walden Edition, p. 410; and in *Poems of Nature*, p. 10.

---

[1] The pagination of the Manuscript Edition is identical with that of the Walden Edition.

Vol. II, No. 2, Oct., 1841.

FRIENDSHIP, "Let such pure hate still underprop,"
p. 204. Signed H. D. T.

Reprinted in *Week*, first edition, p. 300; second edition, p. 304; Riverside Edition, p. 379; Walden Edition, p. 305; and in *Poems of Nature*, p. 26.

Vol. III, No. 1, July, 1842.

NATURAL HISTORY OF MASSACHUSETTS, p. 19. Not signed.

Nominally a review of certain State reports, this was really an original paper drawn largely from the autnor's journal (1837–42).

Reprinted in *Excursions*, first edition, p. 37; Riverside Edition, p. 127; Walden Edition, p. 103.

"GREAT GOD, I ASK THEE FOR NO MEANER PELF," p. 79.
In unsigned article by Emerson entitled "Prayers."

Reprinted in *A Yankee in Canada, with Anti-Slavery and Reform Papers*, p. 120; in *Miscellanies*, Riverside Edition, p. 363; in *Poems of Nature*, p. 121; and in *Excursions, and Poems*, Walden Edition, p. 418.

Vol. III, No. 2, Oct., 1842.

THE BLACK KNIGHT, "Be sure your fate." Signed H. D. T.

Reprinted in *Miscellanies*, p. 361; and as a part of "Independence," in *Poems of Nature*, p. 117, and *Excursions, and Poems*, Walden Edition, p. 416.

THE INWARD MORNING, "Packed in my mind lie all the clothes," p. 198. Signed H. D. T.

Reprinted in *Week*, first edition, p. 308; second edition, p. 311; Riverside Edition, p. 388; Walden Edition, p. 313; and in *Poems of Nature*, p. 58.

FREE LOVE, "My love must be as free," p. 199. Signed H. D. T.

Reprinted in *Week*, first edition, p. 293; second edition, p. 296; Riverside Edition, p. 369; Walden Edition, p. 297; and in *Poems of Nature*, p. 37.

THE POET'S DELAY, "In vain I see the morning rise,"
p. 200. Signed H. D. T.

Reprinted in *Week*, first edition, p. 362; second edition, p. 364; Riverside Edition, p. 453; Walden Edition,
p. 366; and in *Poems of Nature*, p. 73.

RUMORS FROM AN ÆOLIAN HARP, "There is a vale
which none hath seen," p. 200. Signed H. D. T.

Reprinted in *Week*, first edition, p. 181; second edition, p. 185; Riverside Edition, p. 229; Walden Edition,
p. 184; and in *Poems of Nature*, p. 39.

THE MOON, "The full-orbed moon with unchanged
ray," p. 222. Signed T.

Reprinted in *Poems of Nature*, p. 71; and in *Excursions, and Poems*, Walden Edition, p. 406.

TO THE MAIDEN IN THE EAST, "Low in the eastern
sky," p. 222. Unsigned.

Reprinted, in part, in *Week*, first edition, p. 51; second
edition, p. 54; Riverside Edition, p. 58; Walden Edition, p. 46; in full, in *Poems of Nature*, p. 32; and in
Excursions and Poems, Walden Edition, p. 400.

THE SUMMER RAIN, "My books I'd fain cast off, I
cannot read," p. 224. Signed T.

Reprinted in *Week*, first edition, p. 318; second edition,
p. 320; Riverside Edition, p. 397; Walden Edition,
p. 320; and in *Poems of Nature*, p. 64.

VOL. III, No. 3, Jan., 1843.

THE LAWS OF MENU, p. 331. Selected by Thoreau.
Unsigned.

THE PROMETHEUS BOUND [Translation of Æschylus],
p. 363. Signed H. D. T.

Reprinted in *Miscellanies*, Riverside Edition, p. 288,
and in *Excursions, and Poems*, Walden Edition, p. 337.

VOL. III, No. 4, April, 1843.

ANACREON, with translations of eleven poems, p. 484.
Signed H. D. T.

The translations are from the pseudo-Anacreon, and the short essay apparently relates to the same.

Reprinted in *Week*, first edition, p. 236; second edition, p. 238; Riverside Edition, p. 295; Walden Edition, p. 238.

ETHNICAL SCRIPTURES: SAYINGS OF CONFUCIUS, p. 493. Selected by Thoreau. Unsigned.

TO A STRAY FOWL, "Poor bird! destined to lead thy life," p. 505. Signed T.

Reprinted in *Miscellanies*, Riverside Edition, p. 360; in *Poems of Nature*, p. 94; and in *Excursions, and Poems*, Walden Edition, p. 411.

ORPHICS: I, *Smoke*; II, *Haze*, p. 505. Signed T.

"Smoke" reprinted in *Walden*, first edition, p. 271; Riverside Edition, p. 391; Walden Edition, p. 279; and in *Poems of Nature*, p. 69. "Haze" reprinted in *Week*, first edition, p. 227; second edition, p. 229; Riverside Edition, p. 284; Walden Edition, p. 229; and in *Poems of Nature*, p. 70.

DARK AGES, p. 527. Signed T.

Reprinted in *Week*, first edition, p. 159; second edition, p. 164; Riverside Edition, p. 200; Walden Edition, p. 161.

FRIENDSHIP, From Chaucer's Romaunt of the Rose, p. 529. Selected by Thoreau. Unsigned.

VOL. IV, No. 2, Oct., 1843.

ETHNICAL SCRIPTURES: CHINESE FOUR BOOKS, p. 205. Selected by Thoreau. Unsigned.

A WINTER WALK, p. 211. Signed H. D. T.

Reprinted by Mr. Sanborn in the *Commonwealth*, March 27 and April 3, 1863; *Excursions*, first edition, p. 109; Riverside Edition, p. 199; Walden Edition, p. 163.

In a letter dated Sept. 8, 1843, Emerson writes Thoreau: "I mean to send the 'Winter's Walk' to the printer to-morrow for *The Dial*. I had some hesitation about it, notwithstanding its faithful observation and its fine sketches of the pickerel-fisher and of the woodchopper, on account of *mannerism*, an old charge of mine, — as if, by attention, one could get the trick of the rhetoric. . . . By pretty free omissions, however, I have removed my principal objections." Some excised pages of this essay, including a poem, were printed in Mr. Sanborn's *Personality of Thoreau*, and afterward in Mr. Cooke's Introduction to *The Dial*.

VOL. IV, No. 3, Jan., 1844.

HOMER. OSSIAN. CHAUCER. *Extracts from a Lecture on Poetry, read before the Concord Lyceum, November 29, 1843, by Henry D. Thoreau*, p. 290.

Reprinted in *Week*, first edition, pp. 95–99, 362–367, 386–396; second edition, pp. 98–102, 364–369, 387–398; Riverside Edition, pp. 116–122, 453–459, 483–497; Walden Edition, pp. 93–98, 366–371, 391–403.

PINDAR [Fragmentary translations, which the headnote credits to Thoreau], p. 379.

Reprinted, in part, in *Miscellanies*, Riverside Edition, p. 337; and in *Excursions, and Poems*, Walden Edition, p. 375.

Mr. W. K. Bixby of St. Louis has the manuscript of these fragments, including those printed in the succeeding number.

THE PREACHING OF BUDDHA, p. 391. Edited by Thoreau. Unsigned.

ETHNICAL SCRIPTURES: HERMES TRISMEGISTUS, p. 402. Selected by Thoreau. Unsigned.

VOL. IV, No. 4, April, 1844.

HERALD OF FREEDOM, p. 507. Signed H. D. T.

A notice of the anti-slavery journal of that name conducted by Nathaniel P. Rogers in Concord, N. H.

Reprinted in *A Yankee in Canada, with Anti-Slavery and Reform Papers*, p. 206; *Miscellanies*, Riverside Edition, p. 70; *Cape Cod, and Miscellanies*, Walden Edition, p. 306.

FRAGMENTS OF PINDAR, p. 513. Signed T.

Reprinted in *Miscellanies*, Riverside Edition, p. 355; and in *Excursions, and Poems*, Walden Edition, p. 390.

THE BOSTON MISCELLANY.

A WALK TO WACHUSETT, Jan., 1843, vol. 3, p. 31.

As to payment for the article, see *Familiar Letters*, Walden Edition, pp. 83, 84, 102, 103.

Reprinted in *Excursions*, first edition, p. 73; Riverside Edition, p. 163; Walden Edition, p. 133.

THE DEMOCRATIC REVIEW.

THE LANDLORD, Oct., 1843, vol. 13 (Old Series, vol. 44), p. 427.

Reprinted in the [Boston] *Commonwealth* (weekly), March 13, 1863; and in *Excursions*, first edition, p. 97; Riverside Edition, p. 187; Walden Edition, p. 153.

PARADISE (TO BE) REGAINED, Nov., 1843, vol. 13, p. 451.

A review of a book by J. A. Etzler. Written on Staten Island.

Reprinted in *A Yankee in Canada*, etc., p. 182; in *Miscellanies*, Riverside Edition, p. 38; and in *Cape Cod, and Miscellanies*, Walden Edition, p. 280.

GRAHAM'S MAGAZINE.

THOMAS CARLYLE AND HIS WORKS, March, 1847, vol. 30, p. 145; April, 1847, vol. 30, p. 238.

Horace Greeley was Thoreau's agent in placing this article for publication. Thoreau had some difficulty in getting his pay for it, but Greeley finally succeeded in collecting it for him by drawing on Graham for $75. See Sanborn's Life of Thoreau, pp. 218–225.

Reprinted in *A Yankee in Canada*, etc., p. 211; in *Miscellanies*, Riverside Edition, p. 81; and in *Cape Cod, and Miscellanies*, Walden Edition, p. 316.

THE LIBERATOR.

WENDELL PHILLIPS BEFORE THE CONCORD LYCEUM, March 28, 1845. Letter dated March 12, 1845, not signed.

Reprinted in *A Yankee in Canada*, etc., p. 274; in *Miscellanies*, Riverside Edition, p. 76; and in *Cape Cod, and Miscellanies*, Walden Edition, p. 311.

SLAVERY IN MASSACHUSETTS, July 21, 1854. An Address
delivered at the Anti-Slavery Celebration at Framingham, July 4th, 1854.

Made up largely from entries made in Thoreau's Journal at
the time of the rendition of Sims in 1851 and during the discus-
sion of the Anthony Burns affair in May and June, 1854.

Reprinted in *A Yankee in Canada*, etc., p. 97; in *Miscellanies*, p. 171; and in *Cape Cod, and Miscellanies*,
p. 388.

[THE LAST DAYS OF JOHN BROWN], July 27, 1860. In
a report of the Memorial Celebration at North Elba,
N. Y., July 4, 1860. Thoreau's address was read by
the secretary.

Written almost entirely in the Journal at the time of John
Brown's trial and execution.

Reprinted in *A Yankee in Canada*, etc., p. 278; in
Miscellanies, Riverside Edition, p. 237; and in *Cape Cod,
and Miscellanies*, Walden Edition, p. 441.

THE UNION MAGAZINE.

KTAADN AND THE MAINE WOODS, vol. 3, 1848.
No. I. The Wilds of the Penobscot, p. 29 (July).
No. II. Life in the Wilderness, p. 73 (Aug.).
No. III. Boating on the Lakes, p. 132 (Sept.).
No. IV. The Ascent of Ktaadn, p. 177 (Oct.).
No. V. The Return Journey, p. 216 (Nov.).

This series was sold for Thoreau to Mr. Sartain, the pro-
prietor of the *Union Magazine*, by Horace Greeley, who had
previously bought it himself for $25, with the idea of using it in
the *Tribune*. Sartain gave him $75 for it, upon which he handed
over an additional $25 to the author. See Sanborn's Thoreau,
pp. 225–227.

Reprinted in *The Maine Woods*, first edition, p. 1;
Riverside Edition, p. 3; Walden Edition, p. 3.

ÆSTHETIC PAPERS. Edited by Elizabeth P. Pea-body. Boston: The Editor, 1849.

RESISTANCE TO CIVIL GOVERNMENT, p. 189.

Reprinted under the title "Civil Disobedience" in

A Yankee in Canada, etc., p. 123; in *Miscellanies*, Riverside Edition, p. 131; and in *Cape Cod, and Miscellanies*, Walden Edition, p. 356.

PUTNAM'S MONTHLY MAGAZINE.

EXCURSION TO CANADA, vol. 1, 1853.

   i. Concord to Montreal, Jan., p. 54.

   ii. Quebec and Montmorenci, Feb., p. 179; March, p. 321.

   iii. St. Anne, March, p. 322.

CAPE COD, vols. 5 and 6, 1855.

The Shipwreck, June, vol. 5, p. 632.

Stage-Coach Views, p. 637.

The Plains of Nanset [*sic*], July, vol. 6, p. 59.

The Beach, Aug., vol. 6, p. 157.

The notice *To be Continued* is appended to the August installment, but the series was discontinued, and nothing more of *Cape Cod* appeared during Thoreau's lifetime. Mr. Sanborn says it "became the subject of controversy [between author and editor] first as to price, and then as to its tone towards the people of that region." The serial publication of the "Excursion to Canada" was also terminated abruptly, after only three chapters out of the five which the author wrote had been published. The withdrawal of the remaining chapters was on account of a disagreement between the author and the editor of *Putnam's*, Mr. George William Curtis, who, as Thoreau wrote his friend Blake, required the liberty to omit the "heresies" without consulting the author, — an attitude which Mr. Greeley defended on the ground that the articles were unsigned and therefore in a sense editorial. According to Mr. Sanborn it was as a result of a correspondence with Horace Greeley that the Canada and Cape Cod papers were published in *Putnam's Magazine*. It is evident from the printed correspondence that he negotiated the sale of the "Excursion to Canada" for Thoreau; as to the "Cape Cod," we have no explicit information.

The Canada papers were reprinted in *A Yankee in Canada*, etc., pp. 3–63; and in *Excursions*, Riverside Edition, pp. 3–84; Walden Edition, pp. 3–68. The Cape Cod chapters were reprinted in the volume entitled *Cape Cod*, pp. 1–71; Riverside Edition, pp. 1–91; Walden Edition, pp. 3–78.

THE ATLANTIC MONTHLY.

CHESUNCOOK, vol. 2, 1858. i, p. 1 (June); ii, p. 224 (July); iii, p. 305 (Aug.).

The July installment contains the passage in praise of the pine from which the final sentence, "It is as immortal as I am, and perchance will go to as high a heaven, there to tower above me still," was struck out by the editor, James Russell Lowell. It will be remembered that this editorial liberty offended Thoreau, who never again offered anything to the *Atlantic*, though the three succeeding papers were contributed to the magazine by him at the solicitation of Mr. Fields, who had then assumed the editorship.

Reprinted in *The Maine Woods*, first edition, p. 85; Riverside Edition, p. 112; Walden Edition, p. 93.

WALKING, vol. 9, p. 657 (June, 1862).

A considerable part of this essay appears scattered through the *Journal* in the years 1850–52.

Reprinted in *Excursions*, first edition, p. 161; Riverside Edition, p. 251; Walden Edition, p. 205.

AUTUMNAL TINTS, vol. 10, p. 305 (Oct., 1862).

Drawn largely from the journals for 1851–58.

Reprinted in *Excursions*, first edition, p. 215; Riverside Edition, p. 305; Walden Edition, p. 249.

WILD APPLES, vol. 10, p. 513 (Nov., 1862).

Much of this appears scattered through the *Journal*.

Reprinted in *Excursions*, first edition, p. 266; Riverside Edition, p. 356; Walden Edition, p. 290.

These last three articles, Mr. Sanborn informs the compiler, were corrected in proof at least in part by Thoreau during his last illness.

LIFE WITHOUT PRINCIPLE, vol. 12, p. 484 (Oct., 1863).

Largely composed of passages from the Journal written between 1850 and 1855.

Reprinted in *A Yankee in Canada*, etc., p. 248; *Miscellanies*, Riverside Edition, p. 253; and *Cape Cod, and Miscellanies*, Walden Edition, p. 455.

NIGHT AND MOONLIGHT, vol. 12, p. 579 (Nov., 1863).

Much of this essay appears in the earlier part of the *Journal* (1841–54). It is probably an abridged form of a longer essay which Thoreau delivered as a lecture in 1854.

Reprinted in *Excursions*, first edition, p. 307; Riverside Edition, p. 397; Walden Edition, p. 323.

THE WELLFLEET OYSTERMAN, vol. 14, p. 470 (Oct., 1864).

Reprinted in *Cape Cod*, first edition, p. 72; Riverside Edition, p. 92; Walden Edition, p. 79.

THE HIGHLAND LIGHT, vol. 14, p. 649 (Dec., 1864).

Reprinted in *Cape Cod*, first edition, p. 138; Riverside Edition, p. 179; Walden Edition, p. 150.

APRIL DAYS, vol. 41, p. 445 (April, 1878).

Reprinted in *Early Spring in Massachusetts*, Riverside Edition, pp. 294–322.

MAY DAYS, vol. 41, p. 567 (May, 1878).

Reprinted in *Excursions*, Riverside Edition, p. 410.

DAYS IN JUNE, vol. 41, p. 711 (June, 1878).

Reprinted, with the omission of four or five paragraphs, in *Summer*, pp. 1–27.

WINTER DAYS, vol. 55, p. 79 (Jan., 1885).

Reprinted in *Winter*, pp. 81–107.

THE EMERSON-THOREAU CORRESPONDENCE, vol. 69, pp. 577, 736 (May, June, 1892).

The letters from Thoreau were reprinted in *Familiar Letters, passim*.

THOREAU AND HIS ENGLISH FRIEND, THOMAS CHOLMONDELEY, vol. 72, p. 741 (Dec., 1893).

Contains a single letter from Thoreau to Cholmondeley, which was reprinted in *Familiar Letters*, Riverside Edition, p. 295; Walden Edition, p. 249.

A BIT OF UNPUBLISHED CORRESPONDENCE BETWEEN HENRY THOREAU AND ISAAC HECKER, vol. 90, pp. 370–376 (Sept., 1902).

The same article was published in Proceedings of the American Antiquarian Society, N. S., vol. 15, pp. 58–69, Worcester, 1904. The two letters of Thoreau are reprinted in *Familiar Letters*, Walden Edition, pp. 405–408.

THOREAU'S JOURNAL [extracts], vol. 95, pp. 19–29, 227–235, 364–369, 539–547, 680–686 (Jan.–May, 1905).

Selections from the Journal as afterwards printed.

THE EDITOR WHO WAS NEVER AN EDITOR, by Bliss Perry, vol. 100, p. 661 (Nov., 1907).

Contains two letters from Thoreau to F. H. Underwood. Reprinted in the author's *Park-Street Papers*, 1908.

ECHOES OF HARPER'S FERRY. By James Redpath. Boston: *Thayer and Eldridge*. 1860.

A PLEA FOR CAPTAIN JOHN BROWN (read to the citizens of Concord, Mass., Sunday evening, Oct. 30, 1859), p. 16.

Written almost entirely in the Journal during the days immediately following John Brown's raid.

Reprinted in *A Yankee in Canada*, etc., p. 152; in *Miscellanies*, Riverside Edition, p. 197; and in *Cape Cod, and Miscellanies*, Walden Edition, p. 409.

The address was also delivered in Boston as one of the Fraternity course of lectures, Nov. 1, 1859, and was reported in the *Atlas and Daily Bee* and other Boston papers for Nov. 2, but was not printed in full until the appearance of Mr. Redpath's book.   (See also pp. 118, 119.)

REMARKS AT CONCORD ON THE DAY OF THE EXECUTION OF JOHN BROWN (Dec. 2, 1859), p. 439.

A few sentences of this short address appear in the *Journal*.

Reprinted under the title of "After the Death of John Brown" in *Miscellanies*, Riverside Edition, p. 249; and in *Cape Cod, and Miscellanies*, p. 451.

THE NEW-YORK DAILY TRIBUNE.

THE SUCCESSION OF FOREST TREES, Oct. 6, 1860.

An address read before the Middlesex Agricultural Society at

Concord, Sept. 20, 1860. Drawn to some extent from the author's journal (1852–60). An investigation into the planting and growth of wood-lots occupied a large part of Thoreau's time during the autumn of 1860. (See *Journal*.)

Reprinted in *Excursions*, first edition, p. 135; Riverside Edition, p. 225; Walden Edition, p. 184. See also next two items.

TRANSACTIONS OF THE MIDDLESEX AGRICULTURAL SOCIETY FOR THE YEAR 1860. Concord: *Benjamin Tolman*, Printer. 1860.

AN ADDRESS ON THE SUCCESSION OF FOREST TREES, p. 12.

The same address as the foregoing.

"At 2 o'clock, P. M., a procession was formed at the Society's hall, under the efficient direction of N. Henry Warren, Chief Marshal, and proceeded, under the escort of Gilmore's Band, to the Town Hall, where the meeting was called to order by the President, who, after a few remarks, introduced to the audience Mr. Henry D. Thoreau, who delivered a fine address.

"At the close of the brief address of Mr. Thoreau, Gov. Boutwell, President of the Society, congratulated the audience that they had heard an address so plain and practical, and at the same time showing such close observation, and careful study of natural phenomena." — Pages 8 and 9, in report of the 66th Exhibition of the Society, held at Concord, Sept. 20, 1860.

EIGHTH ANNUAL REPORT OF THE SECRETARY OF THE MASSACHUSETTS BOARD OF AGRICULTURE. Abstract of Returns of the Agricultural Societies of Massachusetts for 1860 [bound in with the Report, but with separate title-page and pagination]. Boston: *William White*, Printer to the State. 1861.

SUCCESSION OF FOREST TREES, p. 11.

An "expurgated" reprint of the foregoing address, omitting the humorous passages.

THE COMMONWEALTH (A Boston weekly edited by F. B. Sanborn).

INSPIRATION (verse), June 19, 1863.

Reprinted in *Poems of Nature*, p. 3; and in *Excursions, and Poems*, Walden Edition, p. 396.

THE FUNERAL BELL (verse), July 3, 1863.

Reprinted in *Poems of Nature*, p. 62; and in *Excursions, and Poems*, Walden Edition, p. 405.

TRAVELLING (verse), July 24, 1863.

These lines have not been reprinted in this form. They are as follows: —

> If e'er our minds are ill at ease,
> It is in vain to cross the seas;
> Or when the fates do prove unkind,
> To leave our native land behind;
> The ship becalmed at length stands still,
> The steed will rest beneath the hill;
> But swiftly still our fortunes pace
> To find us out in every place.

With the exception of the first two lines, this appears (with verbal alterations) in the *Week*, as a part of the poem beginning " Though all the fates should prove unkind." The word " out " in the last line was misprinted as " rest " in the *Commonwealth*.

GREECE (verse), July 24, 1863.

Reprinted in *Poems of Nature*, p. 61; and in *Excursions, and Poems*, p. 404. The last four lines appear in the *Week*.

THE DEPARTURE (verse), Aug. 28, 1863.

Reprinted in *Poems of Nature*, p. 112; and in *Excursions, and Poems*, p. 414.

THE FALL OF THE LEAF (verse), Oct. 9, 1863.

Reprinted in *Poems of Nature*, p. 78; and in *Excursions, and Poems*, p. 407.

INDEPENDENCE (verse), Oct. 30, 1863.

Reprinted in *Poems of Nature*, p. 116; and in *Excursions, and Poems*, p. 415.

THE SOUL'S SEASON (verse), Nov. 6, 1863.

Reprinted as the first four stanzas of "The Fall of the Leaf" in *Poems of Nature*, p. 77; and in *Excursions, and Poems*, p. 407.

A MASQUE OF POETS. [Edited by George Parsons Lathrop.] Boston: *Roberts Bros.* 1878. (No Name Series.)

PILGRIMS (verse), p. 168.

Reprinted in *Miscellanies*, p. 359; in *Poems of Nature*, p. 110; and in *Excursions, and Poems*, Walden Edition, p. 413.

SCRIBNER'S MONTHLY.

DAYS AND NIGHTS IN CONCORD, edited by W. E. Channing, vol. 16, p. 721 (Sept., 1878).

Reprinted in *Excursions*, Riverside Edition, p. 438.

[A LETTER OF THOREAU'S TO R. W. EMERSON, DATED MARCH 11, 1842], vol. 17, pp. 352, 353 (March, 1895) in "Thoreau's Poems of Nature," by F. B. Sanborn.

This letter appears not to have been published elsewhere.

THE CRITIC.

THOREAU'S UNPUBLISHED POETRY, by F. B. Sanborn, March 26, 1881, vol. 1, p. 75.

Omnipresence, 4 lines.
Inspiration, 4 lines.
Prayer, 10 lines.
Mission, 4 lines.
Delay, 4 lines.
The Vireo, 4 lines.

From a sheet found in Thoreau's copy of *The Dial*. "Prayer" had appeared in *The Dial*, vol. 3, p. 79 (see p. 65). "The Vireo" was included in the article entitled "Natural History of Massachusetts," contributed to *The Dial* for July, 1842. Besides its several appearances in that article, it was reprinted in *Poems of Nature*, p. 72.

The other four quatrains were reprinted in *Miscellanies*,
Riverside Edition, pp. 363, 364; and in *Excursions, and
Poems*, Walden Edition, pp. 417, 418.

HENRY D. THOREAU. (American Men of Letters.) By F. B. Sanborn. Boston: *Houghton,
Mifflin & Co.* 1882.

To MY BROTHER (verse), p. 176.

Reprinted in *Poems of Nature*, p. 52; and in *Excursions, and Poems*, Walden Edition, p. 403.

CONCORD LECTURES ON PHILOSOPHY. Collected
and arranged by Raymond L. Bridgman.
Cambridge, Mass.: *Moses King.* [1883.]

THE SERVICE: QUALITIES OF THE RECRUIT, p. 124.

Extracts from Thoreau's essay of that title read from
his manuscript by F. B. Sanborn at the Concord School
of Philosophy, Aug. 2, 1882.

Reprinted in *Miscellanies*, Riverside Edition, p. 35; and
in *Cape Cod, and Miscellanies*, Walden Edition, p. 277.
See also p. 37, *The Service*. This volume also contains
extracts from several of Thoreau's letters, pp. 125, 126.

THE PERSONALITY OF THOREAU. B F. B. Sanborn. Boston: *Charles E. Goodspeed.* 1901.

[POEM (17 lines) beginning "Pray, to what earth does this
sweet cold belong," with a paragraph of prose], pp. 31,
32.

From the manuscript of "A Winter Walk"; omitted by
Emerson in printing the essay in *The Dial*.

[EXCERPT FROM A HARVARD JUNIOR FORENSIC ON "THE
COMPARATIVE MORAL POLICY OF SEVERE AND MILD
PUNISHMENTS"], p. 34.

OUR COUNTRY (poem, 47 lines), pp. 64, 65.

Written about 1841. It came to Mr. Sanborn with other
manuscripts from Emerson, and had presumably been
submitted to *The Dial* but rejected.

PROCEEDINGS OF THE AMERICAN ANTIQUARIAN SOCIETY.

See *Atlantic Monthly*, Sept., 1902.

DANIEL RICKETSON AND HIS FRIENDS. Letters, Poems, Sketches, etc. Edited by Anna and Walton Ricketson. Boston: *Houghton, Mifflin & Co.* 1902.

Contains Letters of Thoreau, pp. 31, 32–37, 40, 42–47, 49, 50, 52, 53, 57–60, 66–75, 77, 79, 80, 83–86, 88, 89, 92–94, 106–108, 111–117; and extracts from Thoreau's Journal, pp. 335–356.

The letters are reprinted in *Familiar Letters*, Walden Edition, and the Journal extracts appear in the complete *Journal*.

FIFTH YEAR BOOK. Boston : *The Bibliophile Society*, 1906.

(Printed for members only.)

EARLY LETTER OF THOREAU, DURING AN ABSENCE FROM COLLEGE, pp. 53–56.

A letter to Henry Vose dated Concord, July 5, 1836 (pp. 55, 56), with a note by Mr. Sanborn (pp. 53–55).

APHORISMS BY HENRY D. THOREAU. FRAGMENTS OF OLD UNPUBLISHED JOURNALS RECENTLY DISCOVERED AMONG THOREAU'S PAPERS, pp. 59–64.

VERMONT BOTANICAL CLUB, Bulletin No. 3. Burlington, Vermont. April, 1908.

THOREAU IN VERMONT IN 1856, by Mrs. Elizabeth B. Davenport, p. 36.

Contains extracts from three unpublished letters of Thoreau to Miss Brown of Brattleboro, Vt., with whose father, the Rev. Addison Brown, Thoreau had made a visit in September, 1856. The letters were written in March, 1857, April, 1858, and May, 1859.

BIOGRAPHIES AND OTHER BOOKS RELATING EXCLUSIVELY TO THOREAU

BIOGRAPHIES AND OTHER BOOKS RELATING EXCLUSIVELY TO THOREAU

ALCOTT, LOUISA M.

Thoreau's Flute (verse). Detroit, Mich.: *E.B.Hill.* 1899.
Reprinted from *Atlantic Monthly* for September, 1863.
Square 16mo, pp. 2 (unnumbered).

ANONYMOUS.

Three Letters. Privately Printed by *Alfred W. Hosmer.*
1900.
Square 16mo, pp. 8. Edition limited to forty copies.
Three letters signed. C., giving impressions of Thoreau.

Henry Thoreau's Mother. Lakeland, Mich.: *Edwin B.
Hill.* 1908.
18mo, pp. 13. With Introduction "Anent Sanborn's
Life of Thoreau" (pp. 3–5). Collectanea, No. 2.

A letter written by Mrs. Jean Munroe Le Brun reprinted from the *Boston Daily Advertiser* for Feb. 14,
1883. The Introduction reprints Mr. Sanborn's sonnet
on Thoreau in its two forms, as published in the Concord *Monitor* in May, 1862.

BARTON, W. G.

Thoreau, Flagg, and Burroughs. Reprint from the Historical Collections of the Essex Institute, vol. xxii, p. 53.
8vo, paper, pp. 28.
The essay was read March 16, 1885.

CHANNING, WILLIAM ELLERY.

Thoreau, the Poet-Naturalist. With Memorial Verses.
Boston: *Roberts Bros.* 1873.
16mo, pp. xii, 357.

Part of it was originally published anonymously by Mr. F. B. Sanborn in the Boston *Commonwealth* in eight installments, the first two under the title of *Henry D. Thoreau*, Dec. 25, 1863, and Jan. 1, 1864, the others under the title of *Reminiscences of Henry D. Thoreau, Part Second* and *Part Third*, Jan. 15, 22, and 29, and Feb. 5, 12, and 19, 1864. It contains many and copious extracts from Thoreau's unpublished Journal. Pages 120–186 were, as explained by Mr. Sanborn in his Introduction to the edition of 1902, added by the author for the purpose of enlarging the volume. They were taken in bulk from an old manuscript written for quite a different purpose, containing a medley of passages from the journals of Emerson and Thoreau, together with scraps of recorded conversations and bits written by Channing himself, etc., etc., all without anything to indicate what was to be ascribed to each author. This and all the circumstances attending the writing and publication of the book are interestingly recounted by Mr. Sanborn in the Introduction referred to. Mr. Channing's quotations of Thoreau's Journal are very inaccurate. Fifteen hundred copies were printed.

The Same. New Edition, enlarged. Edited by F. B. Sanborn. Boston: *Charles E. Goodspeed.* 1902.

Large crown 8vo, pp. xx, 397. With portrait of the author.

This edition was based upon a copy of the earlier edition containing Channing's revision and notes. The editor also inserted here and there passages from "the original sketch," made some additions to the "Memorial Poems," indicated the names of the interlocutors in the "Walks and Talks," and supplied a few additional passages from Thoreau's journals and papers.

Two hundred and fifty copies of this edition, with engraved portraits of Channing and Thoreau and four etchings by Sidney L. Smith, were printed on French

hand-made paper by D. B. Updike, The Merrymount
Press, Boston, in November, 1902.

EMERSON, RALPH WALDO.

Thoreau (Biographical Sketch).[1]

Originally read at Thoreau's funeral. Enlarged and
published in the *Atlantic Monthly*, vol. 10, p. 239. Re-
published in *Excursions* (1863), p. 7; in *Miscellanies*,
Riverside Edition, p. 1; and in *A Week on the Concord
and Merrimack Rivers*, Walden Edition, p. xv; also in
Emerson's *Lectures and Biographical Sketches*.

Henry D. Thoreau: Emerson's Obituary. Lakeland,
Mich.: *Edwin B. Hill*. 1904.

18mo, pp. 10. With Note (pp. 7–10). Collectanea, No. 1.

A reprint of the obituary in the *Boston Daily Advertiser* for May 8, 1862.

HIGGINSON, [SAMUEL] STORROW.

Henry D. Thoreau. Reprinted from the *Harvard Magazine* for May, 1862, by *E. B. Hill*, at The Stylus Press,
Detroit, Mich., July 12, 1900.

Square 16mo, pp. [2].

Mr. Higginson's name is misprinted as "Storms."

HOSMER, ALFRED W.

Chronology of the Life of Henry D. Thoreau. Published
by the Author: Concord, Mass. 1895.

Crown 8vo, paper, pp. 4 (unnumbered).

See also p. 81, ANONYMOUS.

HUBBARD, ELBERT.

Little Journeys to the Homes of Great Philosophers:
Thoreau. (Pages 153–189 of the complete book.) East
Aurora, N. Y.: *The Roycrofters*. 1904.

Square 12mo.

Published in London by A. Owen & Co., 1905, with
eight illustrations and illuminated title-page.

---

[1] This has not been published separately, but is included in this list of
Biographies on account of its great biographical importance.

JAPP, A. H.   (H. A. Page, *pseud.*)

Thoreau: His Life and Aims. A Study. London: *Chatto & Windus*. 1878.

Square 16mo, pp. xii, 271. With two woodcuts, the Walden house and Thoreau after Rowse.

The Same. Boston: *James R. Osgood & Co.* 1877. 18mo, pp. xii, 234.

Set up from advance proof-sheets of the English edition.

JONES, SAMUEL ARTHUR.

Thoreau: A Glimpse. A Paper Read before the Unity Club of Ann Arbor, Michigan, on Monday Evening, December 2d, 1889. Supplemented by a Bibliography of Thoreau. Reprint from *The Unitarian* of January, February, and March, 1890. Privately printed. [Ann Arbor, Mich., 1890.]

16mo, pp. 32 (pp. 27–32, Bibliography).

Some Unpublished Letters of Henry D. and Sophia E. Thoreau. Jamaica, N. Y.: Printed on the *Marion Press*, 1899 [1898].

8vo, pp. xxxvi, 86. Six heliotypes.

Besides introductory and connective matter of a biographical and appreciative character by Dr. Jones, this volume contains a letter of J. A. Froude to Thoreau, dated Sept. 3, 1849, six letters from Thoreau to Calvin H. Greene of Rochester, Mich., four letters from Miss Thoreau to Mr. Greene, and extracts from Greene's diary relating to visits to Concord in 1863 and 1874. The initials X. Y. Z. and X. in letters, text, and diary stand for W. E. Channing, and S. is Mr. Sanborn.

One hundred and fifty copies were printed.

Thoreau: A Glimpse. Concord, Mass.: *Albert Lane*, The Erudite Press. 1903.

8vo, pp. [viii], 35. Half-tone portrait from the Worcester daguerreotype.

A revised edition of this essay with an Introductory Note, together with (pp. 25–35) "Thoreau's Inheritance" reprinted from *The Inlander*.

Thoreau. [Anonymous.] Reprinted from *The Inlander* for Feb., 1893, by *E. B. Hill*, at The Stylus Press, Detroit, Mich., June 11, 1900.
Square 16mo, pp. [2].

JONES, SAMUEL ARTHUR (Editor).
Pertaining to Thoreau. Detroit: *Edwin B. Hill*, 1901.
Square 12mo, pp. xviii, 171.

Contains an Introductory Note dated Dec. 27, 1900, and signed S. A. J.; George Ripley's review of the *Week* in the N. Y. *Tribune*, June 13, 1849; Lowell's review in the *Massachusetts Quarterly Review*, Dec., 1849; C. F. Briggs's "A Yankee Diogenes" in *Putnam's Monthly*, Oct., 1854; Edwin Morton's "Thoreau and his Books" in *Harvard Magazine*, Jan., 1855; "Town and Rural Humbugs" in *Knickerbocker Magazine*, March, 1855; "An American Diogenes" in *Chambers's Journal*, Nov. 21, 1857; A. B. Alcott's "The Forester" in the *Atlantic*, April, 1862; Storrow Higginson's "Henry D. Thoreau" in *Harvard Magazine*, May, 1862; John Weiss's paper in *Christian Examiner*, July, 1865; Henry Williams's sketch in *Memorials of the Class of 1837 of Harvard University*.

KNORTZ, KARL.
Ein amerikanischer Diogenes (Henry D. Thoreau). Hamburg: *Verlagsanstalt und Druckerei Actien-Gesellschaft* (vormals *I. F. Richter*). 1899.
12mo, pp. 32.

LE BRUN, MRS. JEAN MUNROE. *See* p. 81, ANONYMOUS.

LYMAN, EMILY R.
Thoreau. Concord, Mass.: Privately printed for *Alfred W. Hosmer*. 1902.
Tall 16mo, pp. 12 (unnumbered).

MARBLE, ANNIE RUSSELL.
　Thoreau: His Home, Friends, and Books. New York:
　　Thomas Y. Crowell & Co. [1902.]
　　8vo, pp. viii, 343. With eleven photogravures.

PAGE, H. A. *See* JAPP, A. H.

PRINZINGER d. J., A.
　Henry D. Thoreau, ein amerikanischer Naturschilderer.
　　Salzburg: *H. Dieter.* 1895.
　　8vo, pp. 16.

RUSSELL, E. HARLOW.
　A Bit of Unpublished Correspondence between Henry
　　D. Thoreau and Isaac T. Hecker. Worcester, Mass.:
　　Press of *Charles Hamilton*, No. 311 Main Street. 1902.
　　8vo, pp. 14.
　Reprinted from Proceedings of the American Anti-
　quarian Society.
　Fifty copies printed.

SALT, HENRY S.
　The Life of Henry David Thoreau. London: *Richard*
　　Bentley & Son. 1890.
　　8vo, pp. x, 315. Portrait after the Rowse crayon. Ap-
　pendix, pp. 299–307. Index, pp. 309–315. Appendix
　on Thoreau's Parentage, Portraits of Thoreau, and
　Bibliography (pp. 300–307).

　Life of Henry David Thoreau. London: *Walter Scott,*
　　Limited. 1896.
　　Square 16mo and crown 8vo, pp. 208, x. In the "Great
　Writers" Series.
　Revised Edition of the 1890 biography, abridged by the
　omission of many quotations. It has a ten-page Biblio-
　graphy by John P. Anderson of the British Museum.

SANBORN, F. B.
　Henry D. Thoreau. Boston: *Houghton, Mifflin & Co.*
　　1882.

16mo, pp. viii, 324. In American Men of Letters Series.
Steel engraving of the Dunshee ambrotype.

Published in London under the imprint of Sampson
Low, Marston, Searle & Rivington, in July, 1882.

Familiar Letters of Henry David Thoreau. Boston:
Houghton, Mifflin & Co. 1894.

Crown 8vo, pp. xii, 483. With portrait. See description, p. 32. This is to a great extent a biography.

The Same. Large-Paper Edition. 8vo.

The Same. Manuscript Edition.

8vo, pp. xvi, 460. With portrait and five other illustrations.

The Same. Walden Edition. 12mo. See descriptions of
all these editions, pp. 32, 33.

The Personality of Thoreau. Boston: *Charles E. Goodspeed,* 1901.

Tall 8vo, pp. [vi], 71.

Limited Edition of 515 copies printed by D. B. Updike. Photogravure and Facsimiles.

SNYDER, HELENA ADELL.

Thoreau's Philosophy of Life. With Special Considera-
tion of the Influence of Hindoo Philosophy. *University of Heidelberg.* [1902.]

8vo, pp. viii, 93.

Pages 87–89, a Chronological Table of events in Thoreau's life; pages 91–93, a list of works cited.

STEWART, GEORGE, JR.

Thoreau: The Hermit of Walden. A Paper read before
the Literary and Historical Society of Quebec, March
7, 1882. Quebec: Printed at the "*Morning Chronicle*"
Office. 1882.

Crown 8vo, paper, pp. 30. Fifty copies printed.

BIBLIOGRAPHIES

THE only bibliographies of Thoreau of any interest or importance to the student or the collector are those by Dr. Samuel A. Jones. Thoreau's books are enumerated in many works on American literature, and several comprehensive American bibliographies give lists of his first editions, but it seems unnecessary to make any detailed mention of these lists here. Dr. Jones's first bibliography was entitled "A Contribution toward a Bibliography of Thoreau." It appeared in *The Unitarian* for March, 1890 (vol. 5, pp. 126–128), and was reprinted in *Thoreau: A Glimpse* (1890), and in the volume of *Thoreau's Thoughts* compiled by H. G. O. Blake (Boston, 1890), where it occupies pages 125–146. For practical purposes it was of course superseded by his more complete book compiled for the Rowfant Club and printed in 1894, — which, however, is out of the reach of most students on account of the small size of the edition, — and by the bibliography which Mr. John P. Anderson of the British Museum furnished for the "Great Writers" edition of Salt's Life of Thoreau (1896). The latter seems to have been taken almost entirely from Dr. Jones's book, though a very few new items were added. The earlier edition (1890) of Salt's Life also contained an eight-page bibliography, for which credit was given to Dr. Jones in the preface. The title and collation of the Rowfant Club volume are as follows: —

[Motto] | BIBLIOGRAPHY | OF HENRY DAVID | THOREAU | With an Outline | of his Life | [*Device*] | Compiled and Chrono- | logically arranged by | Samuel Arthur Jones | Printed for the Rowfant | Club of Cleveland by the | De Vinne Press of New York | MDCCCXCIV.

Crown 8vo, pp. 80. With Portrait. Collation: [i], half-title and number; 1, title; 2, copyright; 3, motto; 4, blank; 5, errata; 6, blank; 7, contents; 8, blank; 9–25, Chronology of Thoreau's Life; 26–31, Contributions to the Dial; 32–36, Contributions to Other Magazines, 1843–62; 37–54, Works; 55–57, The Order of Publication, Contents, and Arrangement of the Two Editions [i. e. original and Riverside editions]; 58, 59, Biographical, 1862–90; 60–67, Ana, 1847–93; 68–76, Reviews, Criticisms, etc., 1849–94; 77, 78, Years and Works; 79, 80, Index of Writers.

Ninety copies printed. The portrait is a photograph of Mr. H. G. O. Blake's Maxham daguerreotype not reversed.

BOOKS CONTAINING CRITICAL AND BIOGRAPHICAL MATTER

BOOKS CONTAINING CRITICAL AND BIOGRAPHICAL MATTER ABOUT THOREAU

ABBOTT, CHARLES C.
Recent Rambles, or In Touch with Nature, pp. 62–69. Philadelphia: *J. B. Lippincott Co.* 1892.
Notes of the Night, and Other Outdoor Sketches, pp. 215–224. New York: *The Century Co.* 1896.
The Freedom of the Fields, pp. 20, 59, 60, 116, 117. Philadelphia: *J. B. Lippincott Co.* 1898 [1897].

ALBEE, JOHN.
In Concord Lectures on Philosophy, p. 67. Cambridge: *Moses King.* [1883.]
Remembrances of Emerson, pp. 18–25, 32. New York: *Robert G. Cooke.* 1901.

ALCOTT, AMOS BRONSON.
Emerson, p. 61. Cambridge: Privately printed. 1865.
Concord Days, pp. 11–20, 137–140, 259–264. Boston: *Roberts Brothers.* 1872.
Ralph Waldo Emerson: An Estimate of his Character and Genius: In Prose and Verse, pp. 55, 56, 61, 66. Boston: *A. Williams & Co.* 1882.
Sonnets and Canzonets, pp. 119, 121. Boston: *Roberts Brothers.* 1882.

ALCOTT, MAY.
Concord Sketches. Boston: *Fields, Osgood & Co.* 1869.
A book of photographs of pencil sketches, unpaged. One of the sketches is of the "Hermitage at Walden Pond."

ALGER, WILLIAM ROUNSEVILLE.
The Solitudes of Nature and of Man, pp. 329–338. Boston: *Roberts Brothers.* 1866.

ALLEN, JAMES LANE.
A Kentucky Cardinal, pp. 66, 67. New York: *Harper & Bros.* 1895 [1894].

ALLIBONE, S. AUSTIN.
A Critical Dictionary of English Literature, vol. 3, p. 2406. Philadelphia: *J. B. Lippincott & Co.* 1871.

AMERICAN ANTIQUARIAN SOCIETY. *See* E. H. RUSSELL.

APPLETONS' CYCLOPÆDIA OF AMERICAN BIOGRAPHY. *See* OCTAVIUS BROOKS FROTHINGHAM.

ARNIM, ELIZABETH (BEAUCHAMP), GRÄFIN VON.
The Solitary Summer, pp. 23-26. New York: *The Macmillan Co.* 1899.

BALL, BENJAMIN W.
The Merrimack River, Hellenics, and Other Poems, pp. 50-54. New York: *G. P. Putnam's Sons.* 1892.

BARTLETT, GEORGE B.
The Concord Guide Book, pp. 60, 63-65. Boston: *D. Lothrop & Co.* [1880.]

Concord, Historic, Literary, and Picturesque, pp. 72-75. Boston: *D. Lothrop & Co.* 1885.

BARTON, W. G.
Thoreau, Flagg, and Burroughs. *In* Essex Institute Historical Collections, vol. 22, pp. 53-80. Salem, Mass. 1885. (Jan., Feb., and Mar., 1885.) *See also* GEORGE J. BREED.

BATES, KATHARINE LEE.
American Literature, pp. 260-265 and Index. New York: *The Macmillan Co.* 1897.

BEERS, HENRY A.
A Century of American Literature, p. 204. New York: *Henry Holt & Co.* 1878.

An Outline Sketch of American Literature, pp. 143-148. New York: *Chautauqua Press.* 1887.

Points at Issue, and Some Other Points. Numerous
references to Thoreau. New York: *The Macmillan
Co.* 1904.

BENSON, ARTHUR CHRISTOPHER.
From a College Window, pp. 259–262. London: *Smith,
Elder & Co.* 1906.
In an essay on the simple life.

BENTON, JOEL.
Persons and Places, pp. 8–17, 69–72, 74–77. New York:
Broadway Publishing Co. 1905.

BESANT, WALTER.
The Eulogy of Richard Jefferies, pp. 221–225. London:
Chatto & Windus. 1888.

BINNS, HENRY BRYAN.
A Life of Walt Whitman. Index. London: *Methuen &
Co.* 1905.

BLAKE, H. G. O.
In Early Spring in Massachusetts: From the Journal of
Henry David Thoreau, pp. iii–vii. Boston: *Houghton,
Mifflin & Co.* 1881.
In Summer: From the Journal of Henry David Thoreau,
pp. iii–v. Boston: *Houghton, Mifflin & Co.* 1884.
In Winter: From the Journal of Henry David Thoreau,
pp. iii–vi. Boston: *Houghton, Mifflin & Co.* 1888
[1887].
In Thoreau's Thoughts, pp. iii–vi. Boston: *Houghton,
Mifflin & Co.* 1890.
In Autumn: From the Journal of Henry David Thoreau,
pp. iii–vi. Boston: *Houghton, Mifflin & Co.* 1892.

BLISS, PORTER C.
In Johnson's New Universal Cyclopædia, vol. 4, p. 842.
New York: *Alvin J. Johnson & Son.* 1878.
In Johnson's (Revised) Universal Cyclopædia, vol. 7,
p. 814. New York: *A. J. Johnson & Co.* 1886.

BLOOD, HENRY AMES.
Selected Poems of Henry Ames Blood, pp. 40–43. Washington, D. C.: *The Neale Publishing Co.* 1901.

A poem entitled "Thoreau: In Memoriam."

BOLLES, FRANK.
Land of the Lingering Snow, pp. 98, 102, 197. Boston: *Houghton, Mifflin & Co.* 1891.

BREED, GEORGE J., *and* WILLIAM G. BARTON.
Songs and Saunterings by a Poet and Naturalist, pp. 1–17. Salem, Mass.: *The Salem Press Publishing and Printing Co.* 1892.

Contains an essay on Thoreau, Flagg, and Burroughs by Mr. Barton, reprinted from the Transactions of the Essex Institute, without the quotations originally included.

BREWSTER, WILLIAM TENNEY. *See* GEORGE RICE CARPENTER.

BRONSON, WALTER C.
A Short History of American Literature, pp. 210–213. Boston: *D. C. Heath & Co.* 1900.

BROWN, THEO.
Letters of Theo. Brown, selected and arranged by Sarah Theo. Brown. Third and Enlarged Edition, pp. 45, 53, 56, 79. Worcester: *Putnam, Davis & Co.* 1898.

Brown was a Worcester man, a friend of H. G. O. Blake and of Thoreau.

BURROUGHS, JOHN.
In Essays from "The Critic," pp. 9–18. Boston: *James R. Osgood & Co.* 1882.

Indoor Studies, pp. 1–42. Boston: *Houghton, Mifflin & Co.* 1889.

In Chambers's Encyclopædia, vol. 10, pp. 184, 185. London and Edinburgh: *William and Robert Chambers.* 1892.

In Library of the World's Best Literature, vol. 25, pp. 14871–14876. New York: *R. S. Peale and J. A. Hill.* 1897.

Literary Values, and Other Papers, pp. 197–202. Boston: *Houghton, Mifflin & Co.* 1902.

Leaf and Tendril, pp. 117–119. Boston: *Houghton, Mifflin & Co.* 1908.

CABOT, JAMES ELLIOT.
A Memoir of Ralph Waldo Emerson, pp. 282–284. Boston: *Houghton, Mifflin & Co.* 1887.

CAPEN, OLIVER BRONSON.
Country Homes of Famous Americans, pp. 67–71. New York: *Doubleday, Page & Co.* 1905.
Reprinted from *Country Life in America.* Illustrated.

CARLYLE, THOMAS.
The Correspondence of Thomas Carlyle and Ralph Waldo Emerson, vol. 2, pp. 130, 131, 185. Boston: *James R. Osgood & Co.* 1883.
In the revised edition the references are on pp. 160, 161, 215.

CARPENTER, EDWARD.
England's Ideal, pp. 13, 14, 16. London: *Swan Sonnenschein, Lowrey & Co.* 1887.

CARPENTER, GEORGE RICE.
American Prose, p. 338. New York: *The Macmillan Co.* 1898.

CARPENTER, GEORGE RICE, *and* WILLIAM TENNEY BREWSTER.
Modern English Prose, p. 479. New York: *The Macmillan Co.* 1904.

CARY, ELIZABETH LUTHER.
Emerson, Poet and Thinker, pp. 126, 138, 139. New York: *G. P. Putnam's Sons.* 1904.

CHADWICK, JOHN WHITE.
In Chambers's Cyclopædia of English Literature, New

Edition by David Patrick, pp. 792–794, 796. Philadelphia: *J. B. Lippincott Co.* 1904 [1903].

CHAMBERS'S ENCYCLOPÆDIA. *See* JOHN BURROUGHS.

CHANNING, WILLIAM ELLERY.
Poems, Second Series, pp. 157, 158.   Boston: *James Munroe & Co.* 1847 [1846].
Near Home: A Poem, pp. 3–6, 30, 31. Boston: *James Munroe & Co.* 1858.
The Wanderer: A Colloquial Poem, pp. 25–37, 47, 48, 56, 61–74. Boston: *James R. Osgood & Co.* 1871.
Poems of Sixty-five Years, Selected and Edited by F. B. Sanborn, pp. xxix–xxxii, xxxv–xxxviii, xli, xlii, 115, 116, 160, 161.   Philadelphia and Concord: *James H. Bentley.* 1902.

See also his *Thoreau, the Poet-Naturalist*, which, besides the biographical matter, contains at the end a number of poems referring more or less particularly to Thoreau.

CHENEY, EDNAH D.
Louisa May Alcott: Her Life, Letters, and Journals, p. 98. Boston: *Roberts Brothers.* 1889.

COLBY, J. ROSE.
Literature and Life in School, p. 78. Boston: *Houghton, Mifflin & Co.* 1906.

CONCORD: A FEW OF THE THINGS TO BE SEEN THERE, *passim.* Concord, Mass.: *The Patriot Press.* 1902.

CONCORD LECTURES ON PHILOSOPHY. *See* JOHN ALBEE.

CONWAY, MONCURE DANIEL.
Emerson at Home and Abroad, pp. 279–289. Boston: *James R. Osgood & Co.* 1882.
Life of Nathaniel Hawthorne (" Great Writers " Series), pp. 96, 165, 201, 213. London: *Walter Scott.* 1890.
Autobiography, Memories, and Experiences. Index. Boston: *Houghton, Mifflin & Co.* 1904.

COOKE, GEORGE WILLIS.

Ralph Waldo Emerson: His Life, Writings, and Philosophy. Index. Boston: *James R. Osgood & Co.* 1881.

Early Letters of George William Curtis to John S. Dwight, *passim.* New York: *Harper & Bros.* 1898.

An Historical and Biographical Introduction to accompany *The Dial* as reprinted in numbers for the Rowfant Club, vol. 1, pp. 65, 72, 117–139. [Privately printed for the Rowfant Club, Cleveland, Ohio.] 1902.

Contains a chapter on "Thoreau as Contributor and Assistant Editor," and letters to Thoreau from Emerson, dated Sept. 8 and Oct., 1843.

The Poets of Transcendentalism: An Anthology, pp. 310, 311. Boston: *Houghton, Mifflin & Co.* 1903.

CUMMINGS, CHARLES A.

In The Memorial History of Boston, edited by Justin Winsor, vol. 3, p. 658. Boston: *James R. Osgood & Co.* 1881.

CURTIS, GEORGE WILLIAM.

In Homes of American Authors, pp. 247, 248, 250, 251, 296, 302. New York: *G. P. Putnam & Co.* 1853 [1852].

From the Easy Chair, pp. 62–66. New York: *Harper & Bros.* 1892 [1891].

Literary and Social Essays, pp. 20, 21, 24–26, 39, 46. New York: *Harper & Bros.* 1894.

Reprinted from *Homes of American Authors.*

DIRCKS, WILL H.

In Walden (The Camelot Series), pp. vii–xxviii. London: *Walter Scott.* 1886.

In A Week on the Concord and Merrimack Rivers (The Camelot Series), pp. v–xviii. London: *Walter Scott.* [1889.]

In Essays and Other Writings of Henry Thoreau (The Camelot Series), pp. vii–xv. London: *Walter Scott.* [1891.]

DOLE, NATHAN HASKELL.

In A Week on the Concord and Merrimack Rivers. New York: *Thomas Y. Crowell & Co.* [1900.] Introduction.

DUYCKINCK, EVERT A. *and* GEORGE L.

Cyclopædia of American Literature, vol. 2, pp. 653–656. New York: *Charles Scribner.* 1855.

EASTWOOD, DOROTHY.

Golden Thoughts from Thoreau. Preface. London: *John Lane.* [1907.]

ELIOT, GEORGE (*pseud.*).

George Eliot's Life, vol. 1, p. 410. Edinburgh and London: *William Blackwood & Sons.* 1885.

In a letter to Miss Sara Hennell dated June 29, 1856.

ELLIOTT, WALTER.

Life of Father Hecker, p. 140. New York: *Columbus Press.* 1891.

Concerning Thoreau's mother.

ELLIS, HAVELOCK.

The New Spirit, pp. 90–99. London: *George Bell & Sons.* 1890.

ELLWANGER, GEORGE H.

Idyllists of the Country-side, pp. 173–218. New York: *Dodd, Mead & Co.* 1895.

EMERSON, EDWARD WALDO.

Emerson in Concord. Index. Boston: *Houghton, Mifflin & Co.* 1889 [1888].

EMERSON, RALPH WALDO.

Lectures and Biographical Sketches, pp. 419–452. Boston: *Houghton, Mifflin & Co.* 1883. *See also* p. 83.

The Correspondence of Thomas Carlyle and Ralph Waldo Emerson, vol. 1, pp. 256, 290, 335. Boston: *James R. Osgood & Co.* 1883.

In the revised edition the references are on pp. 269, 316, 361.

ENCYCLOPÆDIA BRITANNICA, THE. *See* WILLIAM SHARP.

ESSAYS FROM "THE CRITIC." *See* JOHN BURROUGHS and F. B. SANBORN.

ESSEX INSTITUTE HISTORICAL COLLECTIONS. *See* W. G. BARTON.

FEDERN, KARL.
Essays zur Amerikanischen Literatur, pp. 141–159. Halle a. d. S., Germany: *Otto Hendel.* (Preface dated Vienna, 1899.)
An essay entitled "Henry David Thoreau."

FIELDS, ANNIE.
James T. Fields: Biographical Notes and Personal Sketches, pp. 101, 102. Boston: *Houghton, Mifflin & Co.* 1881.

FIELDS, JAMES T.
In Papyrus Leaves, Edited by William Fearing Gill, pp. 31–36. New York: *R. Worthington.* 1880 [1879].
A paper entitled "Our Poet-Naturalist."

FIRST CENTURY OF THE REPUBLIC, THE. *See* EDWIN P. WHIPPLE.

FISHER, MARY.
A General Survey of American Literature, pp. 286–309. Chicago: *A. C. McClurg & Co.* 1899.

FLAGG, WILSON.
The Woods and By-Ways of New England, pp. 392–396. Boston: *James R. Osgood & Co.* 1872.
Halcyon Days, pp. 164–168. Boston: *Estes & Lauriat.* 1881.
The same essay as the above.

FROTHINGHAM, OCTAVIUS BROOKS.
In Appletons' Cyclopædia of American Biography, vol. 6, pp. 100, 101. New York: *D. Appleton & Co.* 1889.

FROUDE, JAMES ANTHONY.
  In Some Unpublished Letters of Henry D. and Sophia
  E. Thoreau, pp. 11–13. Jamaica, N. Y.: Printed on
  the *Marion Press*. 1899 [1898].
  A letter to Thoreau, dated Sept. 3, 1849, praising the *Week*,
  which Thoreau had sent him, and expressing great admiration
  for its author. "When I think of what you are — of what you
  have done as well as what you have written, I have the right to
  tell you that there is no man living upon this earth at present
  whose friendship or whose notice I value more than yours."

GARNETT, RICHARD.
  In Lowell's My Study Windows (The Camelot Classics),
  pp. xiv, xv. London: *Walter Scott*. 1886.
  Life of Ralph Waldo Emerson (" Great Writers " Series),
  pp. 157–159. London: *Walter Scott*. 1888.

GILL, WILLIAM FEARING. *See* JAMES T. FIELDS.

GRAHAM, P. ANDERSON.
  Nature in Books, pp. 66–93. London: *Methuen & Co.*
  1891.

GREENOUGH, CHESTER NOYES. *See* BARRETT WENDELL.

GRISWOLD, HATTIE TYNG.
  Personal Sketches of Recent Authors, pp. 298–315.
  Chicago: *A. C. McClurg & Co.* 1898.

GRISWOLD, RUFUS WILMOT.
  The Prose Writers of America, pp. 657–659. Philadelphia: *Porter & Coates.* [1870.]

HARPER, H. H.
  In The First and Last Journeys of Thoreau, pp. vii–x.
  Boston: *The Bibliophile Society.* 1905.

HARRIS, AMANDA B.
  American Authors for Young Folks, pp. 163–176. Boston: *D. Lothrop Co.* 1887.

HASKINS, DAVID GREEN.
  Ralph Waldo Emerson: His Maternal Ancestors, pp.
  119–122. Boston: *Cupples, Upham & Co.* 1887.

HAWTHORNE, JULIAN.
Nathaniel Hawthorne and his Wife: A Biography. Index. Boston: *James R. Osgood & Co.* 1884.

HAWTHORNE, JULIAN, *and* LEONARD LEMMON.
American Literature: A Text-Book for the Use of Schools and Colleges, pp. 145–148. Boston: *D. C. Heath & Co.* 1891.

HAWTHORNE, NATHANIEL.
Mosses from an Old Manse, p. 19. New York: *Wiley & Putnam.* 1846.

Passages from the American Note-Books, vol. 2, pp. 96–99, 111–113, 122, 123. Boston: *Ticknor & Fields.* 1868.

HIGGINSON, THOMAS WENTWORTH.
Short Studies of American Authors, pp. 22–31. Boston: *Lee & Shepard.* 1880 [1879].

The oft-quoted account given by Thoreau in his Journal of the return of the unsold copies of the *Week* was here printed for the first time.

Margaret Fuller Ossoli (American Men of Letters). Index. Boston: *Houghton, Mifflin & Co.* 1884.

Cheerful Yesterdays. Index. Boston: *Houghton, Mifflin & Co.* 1898.

In George R. Carpenter's American Prose, pp. 338–342. New York: *The Macmillan Co.* 1898.

Studies in History and Letters. Index. Boston: *Houghton, Mifflin & Co.* 1900.

HIGGINSON, THOMAS WENTWORTH, and HENRY WALCOTT BOYNTON.
A Reader's History of American Literature, pp. 191–198 Index. Boston: *Houghton, Mifflin & Co.* 1903.

HILL, EDWIN B.
In Henry D. Thoreau: Emerson's Obituary, pp. 7–10. Lakeland, Mich.: *Edwin B. Hill.* 1904.

In Henry Thoreau's Mother, pp. 3–5. Lakeland, Mich.: *Edwin B. Hill.* 1908.

HOAR, GEORGE FRISBIE.
A Boy Sixty Years Ago, pp. 33-36. Boston: *Perry Mason & Co.*

Autobiography of Seventy Years, vol. 1, pp. 70-72. New York: *Charles Scribner's Sons.* 1903.

HOLMES, OLIVER WENDELL.
Ralph Waldo Emerson (American Men of Letters). Index. Boston: *Houghton, Mifflin & Co.* 1885 [1884].

HOWE, M. A. DE WOLFE.
American Bookmen. Index. New York: *Dodd, Mead & Co.* 1898.

HUBBARD, ELBERT.
Little Journeys to the Homes of Good Men and Great (John Ruskin), p. 63. New York: *G. P. Putnam's Sons.* 1895.
See also p. 83.

HUBERT, PHILIP G., JR.
Liberty and a Living, pp. 171-199. New York: *G. P. Putnam's Sons.* 1889.

HUDSON, W. H.
Birds in a Village, pp. 153, 190. London: *Chapman & Hall.* 1893.

INTERNATIONAL ENCYCLOPÆDIA, THE NEW, vol. 16, p. 701. New York: *Dodd, Mead & Co.* 1904.

JAMES, HENRY, JR.
Hawthorne (English Men of Letters), pp. 93, 94. New York: *Harper & Bros.* 1880 [1879].

The Same. English edition, pp. 96, 97. London: *Macmillan & Co.* 1879.

JONES, SAMUEL ARTHUR.
In Thoreau's Thoughts, edited by H. G. O. Blake, pp. 127-129. Boston: *Houghton, Mifflin & Co.* 1890.

Some Unpublished Letters of Henry D. and Sophia E. Thoreau: A Chapter in the History of a Still-born Book. Prefatory Note. Jamaica, Queensborough, New York: *The Marion Press.* 1899.

JORDAN, DAVID STARR.
The Story of the Innumerable Company, and Other
Sketches, pp. 177–201. San Francisco: *The Whitaker
& Ray Co.* 1896.
The paper entitled "The Last of the Puritans" is an address
on Thoreau and John Brown delivered before the California
State Normal School at San José, 1892. Brown is called the last
of the Puritans.
Imperial Democracy, pp. 277–293. New York: *D. Ap-
pleton & Co.* 1899.
"The Last of the Puritans" reprinted.

KENNEDY, WILLIAM SLOANE.
In Portia's Gardens, pp. 151–153, 212, 213. Boston:
Bradlee Whidden. 1897.

KNORTZ, KARL.
Geschichte der Nordamerikanischen Literatur, vol. 1, pp.
283–293. Berlin: *Hans Lüstenöder.* 1891.

LATHROP, ROSE HAWTHORNE.
Memories of Hawthorne. Index. Boston: *Houghton,
Mifflin & Co.* 1897.

LAUGHLIN, CLARA E.
Stories of Authors' Loves, vol. 1, pp. 295–308. Philadelphia: *J. B. Lippincott Co.* 1902.

LAWTON, WILLIAM CRANSTON.
Introduction to the Study of American Literature, pp.
138–143. New York: *Globe School Book Co.* 1902.

LIBRARY OF AMERICAN LITERATURE, A. *See* ARTHUR STED-
MAN.

LIBRARY OF THE WORLD'S BEST LITERATURE. *See* JOHN
BURROUGHS.

LITERARY AND HISTORICAL SOCIETY OF QUEBEC. *See*
GEORGE STEWART, JR.

LOTHROP, HARRIET MULFORD (Margaret Sidney, *pseud.*).
Old Concord: Her Highways and Byways, pp. 33–39,
62–64, 77–85, 105. Boston: *D. Lothrop Co.* 1888.

LOWELL, JAMES RUSSELL.
A Fable for Critics, p. 32. [New York:] *G. P. Putnam*.
1848.
My Study Windows, pp. 193–209.   Boston: *James R.
Osgood & Co.* 1871.
See also RICHARD GARNETT.

LYMAN, EMILY R.
In Extracts from Thoreau, pp. 3–5.   Philadelphia:
Printed by *J. B. Lippincott Co.* 1899.

MABIE, HAMILTON WRIGHT.
Our New England, p. 3. Boston: *Roberts Brothers*. 1890.
Essays on Nature and Culture, p. 121.   New York:
Dodd, Mead & Co. 1896.
A later edition from the same plates was published in 1904
under the title of *Nature and Culture.*
Backgrounds of Literature, pp. 74, 75, 90.   New York:
The Outlook Co. 1903.

MARBLE, ANNIE RUSSELL.
In Thoreau's Maine Woods, New York: *Thomas Y.
Crowell & Co.* [1906], pp. vii–xv.
In Thoreau's Cape Cod, New York: *Thomas Y. Crowell
& Co.* [1907], pp. v–xiii.

MATTHEWS, BRANDER.
An Introduction to the Study of American Literature,
pp. 184–193. New York: *American Book Co.* 1896.

MERRIAM, C. HART.
The Mammals of the Adirondack Region, p. 139. New
York: *Henry Holt & Co.* 1886.

METCALF, HENRY AIKEN.
In Sir Walter Raleigh, by Henry David Thoreau, pp.
xi–xiv. Boston: *The Bibliophile Society.* 1905.

MILLARD, BAILEY.
Songs of the Press, p. 111. San Francisco: *Elder & Shep-
ard.* 1902.
A sonnet on "Thoreau of Walden."

MITCHELL, DONALD G.
American Lands and Letters: Leather-Stocking to Poe's
"Raven" (vol. 2), pp. 191, 223, 271–282. New York:
Charles Scribner's Sons. 1899.

MORE, PAUL ELMER.
Shelburne Essays, First Series, pp. 1–21. New York:
G. P. Putnam's Sons. 1904.

MORRIS, CHARLES.
Half-Hours with the Best American Authors, p. 39.
Philadelphia: *J. B. Lippincott Co.* [1886.]

MOULTON, CHARLES WELLS, editor.
The Library of Literary Criticism of English and Ameri-
can Authors, vol. 6, pp. 267–278. Buffalo: *The Moulton
Publishing Co.* 1901.

Comment and criticism on Thoreau selected from the writ-
ings of F. B. Sanborn, R. W. Emerson, G. W. Curtis, Louisa
M. Alcott, Moncure D. Conway, W. R. Alger, W. E. Channing,
T. W. Higginson, E. P. Whipple, John Burroughs, Robert
Louis Stevenson, Theodore F. Wolfe, Ina Russelle Warren,
Rose Hawthorne Lathrop, Charles F. Briggs, A. P. Peabody,
E. A. and G. L. Duyckinck, H. S. Salt, F. L. Pattee, Bradford
Torrey, W. D. Howells, Thomas Carlyle, James Russell Lowell,
A. B. Alcott, A. H. Japp, Thomas Hughes, Henry James, Jr.,
James Purves, Alfred H. Welsh, Walter Lewin, Joel Benton,
C. F. Richardson, F. H. Underwood, William Sharp, Philip G.
Hubert, Jr., H. G. O. Blake, Havelock Ellis, P. A. Graham, G. H.
Ellwanger, Brander Matthews, Donald G. Mitchell, Frederick
M. Smith, Barrett Wendell, W. C. Bronson, and Paul E. More.

NELSON'S ENCYCLOPÆDIA, vol. 12, pp. 56, 57. New York:
Thomas Nelson & Sons. 1907.

NICHOL, JOHN.
American Literature: An Historical Sketch, pp. 313–321.
Edinburgh: *Adam & Charles Black.* 1882.

NOBBE, WILHELM.
In Walden, oder Leben in den Wäldern, pp. i–xxiv. Jena
and Leipzig: *Eugen Diederichs.* 1905.

PATTEE, FRED LEWIS.
A History of American Literature, pp. 221–227, 461. Boston: *Silver, Burdett & Co.* 1896.

PEABODY MUSEUM OF AMERICAN ARCHÆOLOGY AND ETHNOLOGY.
Third Annual Report, pp. 6, 7. Boston: Press of *A. A. Kingman.* 1870. Contained in vol. 1 of Reports of the Peabody Museum; Cambridge, 1876.
Concerning Thoreau's collection of Indian implements, which was deposited in the museum.

PERRY, BLISS.
Walt Whitman: His Life and Work. Index. Boston: *Houghton, Mifflin & Co.* 1906.

PORTRAITS AND BIOGRAPHICAL SKETCHES OF TWENTY AMERICAN AUTHORS, 2 pp. of biography and a woodcut portrait (book unpaged). Boston: *Houghton, Mifflin & Co.* 1887.
Extra number B of Riverside Literature Series.

POWYS, JOHN COWPER.
Syllabus of a Course of Six Lectures on Representative American Writers. Philadelphia: *The American Society for the Extension of University Teaching.* 1904.

RAYMOND, WALTER.
In Walden, Everyman's Library, pp. vii–xii. London: *J. M. Dent & Co.* New York: *E. P. Dutton & Co.* 1908.

RICHARDSON, CHARLES F.
American Literature, vol. 1, pp. 384–395. New York: *G. P. Putnam's Sons.* 1887 [1886].

RICKETSON, ANNA *and* WALTON.
Daniel Ricketson and his Friends. Boston: *Houghton, Mifflin & Co.* 1902.
Devoted largely to Thoreau. Contains a fine reproduction of the Dunshee ambrotype of Thoreau, a half-tone of a pencil

sketch of Thoreau by D. Ricketson, a photographic reproduction of W. Ricketson's bust of Thoreau, and a facsimile of one of Thoreau's letters.

RICKETSON, DANIEL.

The Autumn Sheaf: A Collection of Miscellaneous Poems, pp. 198–201, 209–211. New Bedford: Published by the Author, 1869.

In Daniel Ricketson and his Friends (cited on p. 110), pp. 11–21 (Sketch and Poem), and many references.

RICKETT, ARTHUR.

The Vagabond in Literature, pp. 89–114. London: *J. M. Dent & Co.* 1906.

ROBBINS, REGINALD C.

Poems of Personality, pp. 134–141. Cambridge: Printed at the *Riverside Press.* 1904.

ROBERTS, CHARLES G. D.

In Thoreau's Walden, New York: *Thomas Y. Crowell & Co.* [1899.] Introduction.

ROBERTS, HARRY.

In Life and Friendship, selected from Essays and Diaries of Henry D. Thoreau. Prefatory Note. London: *Anthony Treherne & Co.* 1904.

ROBERTSON, JOHN M.

Modern Humanists, p. 133. London: *Swan Sonnenschein & Co.* 1891.

RUSSELL, E. HARLOW.

In Proceedings of the American Antiquarian Society, n. s., vol. 15, pp. 58–69. Worcester. 1904.

" A Bit of Unpublished Correspondence between Henry D. Thoreau and Isaac T. Hecker." The same article that appeared in the *Atlantic*, Sept., 1902.

SALT, HENRY S.

Literary Sketches, pp. 124–166. London: *Swan Sonnenschein, Lowrey & Co.* 1888.

In Anti-Slavery and Reform Papers, with an Introductory Note, pp. 1–20.   London: *Swan Sonnenschein & Co.* 1890.

Richard Jefferies: A Study.   Numerous references to Thoreau.   London: *Swan Sonnenschein & Co.* 1893.

In Selections from Thoreau, pp. v–xx.   London: *Macmillan & Co.* 1895.

SALT, HENRY S., *and* FRANK B. SANBORN.
In Thoreau's Poems of Nature, pp. xi–xix.   Boston: *Houghton, Mifflin & Co.*   London: *John Lane.* 1895.

SANBORN, FRANKLIN B.
Memoirs of John Brown, pp. 45, 50.   Concord, Mass. 1878.

In Essays from "The Critic," pp. 71–78.   Boston: *James R. Osgood & Co.* 1882.

The Life and Letters of John Brown.   Index.   Boston: *Roberts Brothers.* 1885.

Ralph Waldo Emerson (Beacon Biographies), pp. 56, 80, 93, 94, 126–128, 130.   Boston: *Small, Maynard & Co.* 1901.

In The Service, by Henry David Thoreau, pp. vii–xi, 29–31 (Introduction and Notes).   Boston: *Charles E. Goodspeed.* 1902.

The Personality of Emerson, *passim.*   Boston: *Charles E. Goodspeed.* 1903.

New Hampshire Biography and Autobiography, pp. 60, 62, 67, 68, 77.   Concord, N. H.: Privately printed, 1905.

Written for the *Granite Monthly*, but the part relating to Thoreau never appeared there, owing to the suspension of the magazine for a year.

John Brown and his Friends, pp. 7, 9, 13–15, 24.   Privately printed for the author, 1905.

A chapter from *New Hampshire Biography and Autobiography.*

In Sir Walter Raleigh, by Henry David Thoreau, pp. 1–15, 102, 106. Boston: *The Bibliophile Society.* 1905.

In The First and Last Journeys of Thoreau, vol. 1, pp. xi–xxxix, 1–7, 30–32, 49–53, 61–63, 117, 121–126, 141, 142; vol. 2, pp. 7–12, 95, 120–127. Boston: *The Bibliophile Society.* 1905.

In Fifth Year Book, pp. 53–55. Boston: *The Bibliophile Society.* 1906.

SANBORN, F. B., *and* WILLIAM T. HARRIS.

A. Bronson Alcott: His Life and Philosophy. Index. Boston: *Roberts Brothers.* 1893.

SCUDDER, HORACE E.

American Prose, pp. 296–301. Boston: *Houghton, Mifflin & Co.* 1880. (Revised Edition, 1891, pp. 306–310.)

Masterpieces of American Literature, pp. 161–165. Boston: *Houghton, Mifflin & Co.* 1891.

Introductory Notes to the Riverside Editions of the *Week, Walden, The Maine Woods, Cape Cod, Excursions,* and *Miscellanies.*

These were reprinted, with revision, in the Manuscript and Walden editions.

SEARS, LORENZO.

American Literature in the Colonial and National Periods, pp. 338–347. Boston: *Little, Brown & Co.* 1902.

SHARP, WILLIAM.

In The Encyclopædia Britannica, Ninth Edition, vol. 23, pp. 313, 314. Edinburgh: *Adam and Charles Black.* 1888.

SIDNEY, MARGARET. *See* HARRIET MULFORD LOTHROP.

STANLEY, HIRAM M.

Essays on Literary Art, pp. 113–126. London: *Swan Sonnenschein & Co.* 1897.

A paper on "Thoreau as a Prose Writer."

STEARNS, FRANK PRESTON.
The Life and Genius of Nathaniel Hawthorne, pp. 163–
165, 169, 193. Philadelphia: *J. B. Lippincott Co.* 1906.
The Life and Public Services of George Luther Stearns,
pp. 181, 222. Philadelphia: *J. B. Lippincott Co.* 1907.

STEDMAN, ARTHUR.
In A Library of American Literature, vol. 11, pp. 594,
595. New York: *Charles L. Webster & Co.* 1890.

STEVENSON, A.
Concord and its Philosophers, pp. 3–6.
Reprinted from Proceedings of the 39th Annual Convention
of the Ontario Educational Association, held in Toronto in
April, 1900.

STEVENSON, ROBERT LOUIS.
Familiar Studies of Men and Books, pp. xix–xxiii, 129–
171. London: *Chatto & Windus.* 1882.
The Letters of Robert Louis Stevenson to his Family and
Friends, edited by Sidney Colvin. Index. New York:
Charles Scribner's Sons. 1899.

STEWART, GEORGE, JR.
Thoreau: The Hermit of Walden. In Transactions of the
Literary and Historical Society of Quebec, Sessions of
1881–82, pp. 121–150. Quebec. 1882.

SWAYNE, JOSEPHINE LATHAM.
The Story of Concord told by Concord Writers. Index.
Boston: *The E. F. Worcester Press.* 1906 [1905].

SWIFT, LINDSAY.
Brook Farm: Its Members, Scholars, and Visitors, p. 102.
New York: *The Macmillan Co.* 1900.
Literary Landmarks of Boston, p. 46. Boston: *Houghton,
Mifflin & Co.* 1903.

TAPPAN, EVA MARCH.
A Short History of England's and America's Literature,
pp. 306–310. Boston: *Houghton, Mifflin & Co.* 1906.

A Short History of America's Literature, pp. 48–52.
Boston: *Houghton, Mifflin & Co.* 1907.

A part of the preceding book repaged.

TORREY, BRADFORD.

In Walden, Holiday Edition, vol. 1, pp. ix–xliii. Boston:
Houghton, Mifflin & Co. 1897.

The Clerk of the Woods, pp. 127–134. Boston: *Houghton, Mifflin & Co.* 1903.

" A Text from Thoreau."

In Thoreau's Journal, vol. 1, pp. xix–li. Boston: *Houghton, Mifflin & Co.* 1906.

Reprinted, with revision, from the *Atlantic Monthly.*

Friends on the Shelf, pp. 91–150. Boston: *Houghton,
Mifflin & Co.* 1906.

Two essays, one entitled "Thoreau," the other, "Thoreau's
Demand upon Nature."

TOWNSEND, HARRIET A.

In Touch with Thoreau. Foreword. Buffalo: Privately
printed. 1907.

A short poem prefixed to a Thoreau year-book.

TRAUBEL, HORACE.

With Walt Whitman in Camden (March 28–July 14,
1888) [vol. 1], pp. 212, 213, 231, 314, 335, 448. Boston:
Small, Maynard & Co. 1906.

With Walt Whitman in Camden (July 16, 1888–October
31, 1888) [vol. 2], pp. 52, 329. New York: *D. Appleton & Co.* 1908.

All the references are to quotations from Whitman's conversation, except p. 314 of vol. i, where W. D. O'Connor, in a letter,
quotes Prof. Eben J. Loomis indirectly.

TRENT, WILLIAM P.

A History of American Literature, 1607–1865, pp. 337–
346 (see also Index). New York: *D. Appleton & Co.*
1903.

A Brief History of American Literature, pp. 111–116 (see also Index). New York: *D. Appleton & Co.* 1904.

TRIGGS, OSCAR LOVELL.

Browning and Whitman: A Study in Democracy, pp. 34–36. London: *Swan Sonnenschein & Co.* 1893.

TUCKERMAN, HENRY T.

A Complete Manual of English Literature, by Thomas B. Shaw, with a Sketch of American Literature by Henry T. Tuckerman, p. 532. New York: *Sheldon & Co.* 1867.

UNDERWOOD, FRANCIS H.

A Hand-Book of English Literature: American Authors, p. 414. Boston: *Lee & Shepard.* [1872.]
The running title is "Hand-Book of American Authors."

The Builders of American Literature, First Series, pp. 213–216. Boston: *Lee & Shepard.* 1893.

VINCENT, LEON H.

American Literary Masters, pp. 321–333. Boston: *Houghton, Mifflin & Co.* 1906.

WATKINS, THOMAS COKE.

Henry D. Thoreau: A Little Book of Nature Themes, pp. vii–x. Portland: *Thomas B. Mosher.* 1906.

WATTS-DUNTON, THEODORE.

In Walden. London: *Henry Frowde* [1906]. Introduction.

WEISS, JOHN.

Poem read at the Annual Dinner of the Class of Eighteen Hundred and Thirty-Seven, February 26, 1874, pp. 5, 6. Boston: Press of *W. L. Deland.* 1874.

WELSH, ALFRED H.

Development of English Literature and Language, vol. 2, pp. 409–414. Chicago: *S. C. Griggs & Co.* 1882.

A Digest of English and American Literature, p. 291. Chicago: *S. C. Griggs & Co.* 1890.

WENDELL, BARRETT.
A Literary History of America, pp. 332–337 (see also Index). New York: *Charles Scribner's Sons.* 1900.

WENDELL, BARRETT, *and* CHESTER NOYES GREENOUGH.
A History of Literature in America, pp. 269–274. New York: *Charles Scribner's Sons.* 1904.

WHIPPLE, EDWIN P.
In The First Century of the Republic, p. 389. New York: *Harper & Bros.* 1876.
Article on "A Century of American Literature."
Recollections of Eminent Men, pp. 134, 135. Boston: *Ticknor & Co.* 1887 [1886].
American Literature, and Other Papers, pp. 111, 112. Boston: *Ticknor & Co.* 1887.

WHITEING, RICHARD.
In Walden. London: *Blackie & Son.* [1906.] Introduction.

WHITMAN, WALT.
Specimen Days & Collect, pp. 189–191. Philadelphia: *Rees Welch & Co.* 1882.
See also HORACE TRAUBEL.

WILLIAMS, HENRY.
Memorials of the Class of 1837 of Harvard University, pp. 37–43. Printed for the Class. Boston: *Geo. H. Ellis.* 1887.
The sketch of Thoreau is reprinted in S. A. Jones's *Pertaining to Thoreau*, 1901.

WILSON, RUFUS ROCKWELL.
New England in Letters, pp. 99–105, 109, 110, 112. New York: *A. Wessels Co.* 1904.

WINSOR, JUSTIN. *See* CHARLES A. CUMMINGS.

WOLFE, THEODORE F.
Literary Shrines; the Haunts of some Famous American

Authors. Index. Philadelphia: *J. B. Lippincott Co.* 1895.

WOODBERRY, GEORGE EDWARD.
Ralph Waldo Emerson (in English Men of Letters), pp. 68, 96, 97. New York: *The Macmillan Co.* 1907.

WOODBURY, CHARLES J.
Talks with Ralph Waldo Emerson, pp. 71, 76–95. London: *Kegan Paul, Trench, Trübner & Co.* 1890.

WRIGHT, MARGARET B.
Hired Furnished, being Certain Economical Housekeeping Adventures in England, pp. 126–137. Boston: *Roberts Brothers.* 1897.

About Thoreau's Jersey relatives, dead and living.

NEWSPAPER AND PERIODICAL ARTICLES CONCERNING THOREAU AND HIS WORKS

NEWSPAPER AND PERIODICAL AR-
TICLES CONCERNING THOREAU
AND HIS WORKS

1837

HARVARD COMMENCEMENT PART.

Order of Exercises for Commencement, xxx *August,* MDCCCXXXVII.
Exercises of Candidates for the Degree of Bachelor of Arts.
4. A Conference. "The Commercial Spirit of Modern Times,
considered in its Influence on the Political, Moral, and Literary Character of a Nation."

> CHARLES WYATT RICE, *Brookfield.*
> DAVID HENRY THOREAU, *Concord.*
> HENRY VOSE, *Dorchester.*

1840

ADVERTISEMENT OF CONCORD ACADEMY.

Concord Freeman, March 20.
The advertisement is signed by John Thoreau, Jr. "Henry
D. Thoreau will continue to assist in the Department of the
languages."

1843

ADVERTISEMENT OF CONCORD LYCEUM.

Concord Freeman, February 10.
The list of lecturers includes Thoreau for February 8. This
and the preceding advertisement, as well as the following report,
are in the Hosmer collection in Concord. The advertisements
doubtless also appeared in other numbers of the *Freeman.*

REPORT OF THOREAU'S LECTURE IN CONCORD LYCEUM,
February 8, 1843.

Concord Freeman, February 10.
The lecture was on Sir Walter Raleigh, and was probably

the essay printed for the Bibliophile Society in 1905 from the manuscript owned by Mr. W. K. Bixby. See pp. 40, 41.

1849

H. D. THOREAU'S BOOK. [George Ripley.]
>*New York Tribune*, June 13; also in the *New York Weekly Tribune* for June 16, 1849.
>Reprinted in S. A. Jones's *Pertaining to Thoreau*, 1901. The reviewer praises the literary quality of the *Week*, but condemns the author's pantheism.

NOTICE OF A WEEK ON THE CONCORD AND MERRIMACK RIVERS.
>*Godey's Lady's Book*, September, vol. 39, p. 223.
>This notice is worth quoting in full:—
>"Those who have read 'Margaret Smith's Journal,' will be at no loss in settling the authorship of this clever and interesting work. Mr. Whittier touches all his themes with the true poet's wand; all show forms of beauty and gleams of light that, like the sunbeams on the far-off mountain, make the cold and rugged landscape appear soft and charming. It is just the book to read in the idleness of summer, when wishing to enjoy the pleasures of journeying, without the inconvenience which the actual packing up and going off in hot steamboats and dusty cars occasion. Read it, and see."

REVIEW OF THE WEEK.
>*Athenæum*, October 27, p. 1086.
>A short and slighting notice.

REVIEW OF THE WEEK. [James Russell Lowell.]
>*Massachusetts Quarterly Review*, December, vol. 3, pp. 40–51.
>Reprinted in S. A. Jones's *Pertaining to Thoreau*, 1901.

1853

EMERSON'S CLUB. [George William Curtis.]
>[Boston] *Commonwealth* (Daily), May 19.
>"The inflexible Henry Thoreau, a scholastic and pastoral Orson, then living among the blackberry pastures of Walden pond," etc. Reprinted in *Homes of American Authors*, pp. 250, 251.

1854

REVIEW OF WALDEN.
Christian Register, August 26.

A "CRITICAL NOTICE" OF WALDEN. [A. P. Peabody.]
North American Review, October, vol. 79, p. 536.
A brief but not wholly unappreciative paragraph.

A YANKEE DIOGENES. [Charles Frederick Briggs.]
Putnam's Monthly Magazine, October, vol. 4, pp. 443–448.
A review of *Walden*. Reprinted in S. A. Jones's *Pertaining to Thoreau*, 1901.

WALDEN.
Harvard Magazine, December, vol. 1, p. 45.

1855

THOREAU AND HIS BOOKS. [Edwin Morton.]
Harvard Magazine, January, vol. 1, pp. 87–99.
Reprinted in S. A. Jones's *Pertaining to Thoreau*, 1901.

TOWN AND RURAL HUMBUGS.
Knickerbocker Magazine, March, vol. 45, pp. 235–241.
A comparison and contrast of *Walden* with P. T. Barnum's Autobiography. Thoreau is incidentally called a rural humbug, while Barnum is characterized as a town humbug. The review is favorable to Thoreau in the main, however, in spite of the absurdity of associating him with Barnum. Reprinted in S. A. Jones's *Pertaining to Thoreau*, 1901.

1856

REVIEW OF WALDEN. [Marian Evans (afterwards known as George Eliot).]
Westminster Review, January, vol. 65 (9 N. S.), pp. 302, 303.
This review has apparently never been reprinted, and it is worth quoting in full : —
"In a volume called *Walden; or, Life in the Woods*, published last year, but quite interesting enough to make it worth while for us to break our rule by a retrospective notice — we have a bit of pure American life (not the 'go a-head' species, but its opposite pole), animated by that energetic, yet calm spirit

of innovation, that practical as well as theoretic independence of formulæ, which is peculiar to some of the finer American minds. The writer tells us how he chose, for some years, to be a stoic of the woods; how he built his house; how he earned the necessaries of his simple life by cultivating a bit of ground. He tells his system of diet, his studies, his reflections, and his observations of natural phenomena. These last are not only made by a keen eye, but have their interest enhanced by passing through the medium of a deep poetic sensibility; and, indeed, we feel throughout the book the presence of a refined as well as a hardy mind. People — very wise in their own eyes — who would have every man's life ordered according to a particular pattern, and who are intolerant of every existence the utility of which is not palpable to them, may pooh-pooh Mr. Thoreau and this episode in his history, as unpractical and dreamy. Instead of contesting their opinion ourselves, we will let Mr. Thoreau speak for himself. There is plenty of sturdy sense mingled with his unworldliness."

Then follow extracts, the last of which is prefaced by the words, "We can only afford one more extract, which, to our minds, has great beauty." This is the passage in Chapter IV beginning "I did not read books the first summer; I hoed beans."

1857

AN AMERICAN DIOGENES.

Chambers's Journal, November 21, vol. 8, pp. 330–332.

A review of *Walden*, cribbed in part from the *Knickerbocker* article entitled "Town and Rural Humbugs," from which, besides the absurd comparison with P. T. Barnum, the opening sentences with their reference to Diogenes are borrowed. Reprinted in S. A. Jones's *Pertaining to Thoreau*, 1901.

1859

[REPORT OF THOREAU'S "FRATERNITY LECTURE" ON JOHN BROWN, AND EDITORIAL COMMENT ON THE SAME.]

[Boston] *Atlas and Daily Bee*, November 2.

"Presents the views of a fanatic." In delivering this "Fifth Fraternity Lecture" Thoreau was a volunteer substitute for Frederick Douglass. See also p. 74.

[REPORT OF THOREAU'S "FRATERNITY LECTURE" ON
JOHN BROWN.]
Boston Journal, November 2.
"The lecture occupied an hour and a half and was well
received."

[A REPORT, SIGNED C. K. W., OF THOREAU'S "FRA-
TERNITY LECTURE" ON JOHN BROWN.]
Liberator, November 4, vol. 29, p. 174.
The subject was "Captain John Brown of Ossawattomie."
"A very large audience listened to this lecture, crowding the
hall half an hour before the time of its commencement, and
giving hearty applause to some of the most energetic expres-
sions of the speaker."

1860

[A REPORT OF THE JOHN BROWN MEMORIAL CELEBRA-
TION AT NORTH ELBA, N. Y., July 4, 1860.]
Liberator, July 27, vol. 30, p. 118.
Mr. R. J. Hinton, the secretary of the meeting, read Tho-
reau's address (afterwards published as "The Last Days of
John Brown"), prefacing the reading with appreciative re-
marks about Thoreau's action in coming out strongly for
Brown.

1862

THE FORESTER. [A. Bronson Alcott.]
Atlantic, April, vol. 9, pp. 443–445.
Reprinted in S. A. Jones's *Pertaining to Thoreau*, 1901.

HENRY D. THOREAU. [Storrow Higginson.]
Harvard Magazine, May, vol. 8, pp. 313–318.
Reprinted in S. A. Jones's *Pertaining to Thoreau*, 1901. An
appreciation of Thoreau by a young man who, as a boy in
Concord, knew him and was encouraged and helped by him in
natural history pursuits. It closes with a blank-verse poem.

[OBITUARY.] E. [R. W. Emerson].
Boston Daily Advertiser, May 8.
Reprinted by Edwin B. Hill at Lakeland, Mich., 1904, with
a note by Mr. Hill.

THOREAU [sonnet]. [F. B. Sanborn.]
The Monitor (Concord, Mass.), May 10, vol. 1, p. 28.
Reprinted with corrections in the issue of May 24, vol. 1, p. 46.

[OBITUARY.]
Christian Register, May 17.

WALDEN. [S. Ripley Bartlett.]
The Monitor (Concord, Mass.), May 17, vol. 1, pp. 33, 34.

[NOTICE OF THE 1862 EDITION OF WALDEN.]
The Monitor (Concord, Mass.), June 7, vol. 1, p. 53.

WALDEN (verse). D. R. [Daniel Ricketson].
Liberator, May 23.

HENRY DAVID THOREAU (sonnet). F. B. S[anborn].
Liberator, May 23.
The sonnet as it appeared when published the second time in the Concord *Monitor*, May 24, 1862.

[REMINISCENCES OF THOREAU.] [George William Curtis.]
Harper's Monthly, July, vol. 25, pp. 270, 271.

THOREAU. R. W. Emerson.
Atlantic, August, vol. 10, pp. 239–249.
This is Emerson's well-known biographical sketch of Thoreau, which was read at Thoreau's funeral.

1863

[EDITORIAL IN REGARD TO REPRINTING CERTAIN OF THOREAU'S WRITINGS.]
[Boston] *Commonwealth*, March 13.
With a list of Thoreau's periodical publications "prepared by himself shortly before his death."

THOREAU [poem]. D. A. Wasson.
[Boston] *Commonwealth*, April 17.

THOREAU'S FLUTE [poem]. Louisa M. Alcott.
Atlantic, September, vol. 12, pp. 280, 281.

WALDEN [poem]. John A. Dorgan.
[Boston] *Commonwealth*, September 25.

REVIEW OF EXCURSIONS.
[Boston] *Commonwealth*, October 23.

1864

REVIEW OF THE MAINE WOODS.
New York Times, June 6.

REVIEW OF THE MAINE WOODS.
[Boston] *Commonwealth*, June 10.

REVIEW OF THE MAINE WOODS. [T. W. Higginson.]
Atlantic, September, vol. 14, pp. 386, 387.

AN AMERICAN ROUSSEAU.
Saturday Review, December 3, vol. 18, pp. 694, 695.
A review of *Excursions*.

1865

REVIEW OF CAPE COD. [T. W. Higginson.]
Atlantic, March, vol. 15, p. 381.

CAPE COD.
[Boston] *Commonwealth*, March 25.

THOREAU. [John Weiss.]
Christian Examiner, July, vol. 79, pp. 96–117.
Reprinted in S. A. Jones's *Pertaining to Thoreau*, 1901.

WALDEN POND [poem]. Emma Mortimer Babson.
[Boston] *Commonwealth*, July 22.

REVIEW OF LETTERS TO VARIOUS PERSONS.
The Radical (Boston), September, vol. 1, p. [32].

REVIEW OF LETTERS TO VARIOUS PERSONS. [T. W. Higginson.]
Atlantic, October, vol. 16, pp. 504, 505.

REVIEW OF LETTERS TO VARIOUS PERSONS. [J. R. Lowell.]
North American Review, October, vol. 101, pp. 597–608.
Purporting to be simply a review of the *Letters*, this is really

an essay on Thoreau and his works. It was reprinted in *My Study Windows* under the caption "Thoreau." This essay is included in William Morton Payne's *American Literary Criticism* (New York, 1904) as a specimen of Lowell's work.

1866

THOREAU. [Moncure D. Conway.]
Fraser's Magazine, April, vol. 73, pp. 447–465.
Reprinted in *Eclectic Magazine*, August, 1866, vol. 67, pp. 180–195; and in *Every Saturday*, June 16, 1866, vol. 1, pp. 662–664.

THE HERMIT OF CONCORD. W. R. Alger.
The Monthly Religious Magazine, June, vol. 35, pp. 382–389.

1869

[REMINISCENCES OF THOREAU.] [George William Curtis.]
Harper's Monthly, February, vol. 38, p. 415.

1873

REVIEW OF CHANNING'S THOREAU.
Worcester Spy, September 16.

REVIEW OF CHANNING'S THOREAU.
The Monthly Religious Magazine, October, vol. 50, pp. 383, 384.

REVIEW OF CHANNING'S THOREAU.
Christian Register, November 8.

1874

HENRY THOREAU, THE POET-NATURALIST.
British Quarterly, January, vol. 59, pp. 181–194.
Reprinted in *Littell's Living Age*, March 14, 1874, vol. 120, pp. 643–650; and in *Eclectic Magazine*, March, 1874, vol. 82, pp. 305–312.

MR. WILLIAM ELLERY CHANNING'S "THOREAU."
Nation, January 8, vol. 18, pp. 29, 30.

A SUMMER RAMBLE TO THE HERMIT-HOME OF THOREAU.
E. A. R.
Boston Journal, July 3.

1875

THOREAU AND WILSON FLAGG. Mrs. L. A. Millington.
Old and New [Boston], April, vol. 11, pp. 460–464.

CONCORD BOOKS. Miss Hannah R. Hudson.
Harper's Monthly, June, vol. 51, pp. 18–32.

1877

EVENINGS IN THE LIBRARY: No. 2, EMERSON. Geo.
Stewart, Jr.
Belford's Magazine, January, vol. 1, pp. 222–234.
    A virulent criticism of Thoreau on pp. 231, 232. Mr. Stephen H. Wakeman has an autograph letter of Emerson to Mr. Stewart, taking exception to this attack upon Thoreau.

THOREAU'S HERMITAGE. A. B. H. [Amanda B. Harris].
New York Weekly Evening Post, January 31.

CONCORD AUTHORS CONTINUED. A. M. [Alfred Munroe].
Richmond County Gazette [Stapleton, N. Y.], August 15.

THOREAU: HERMIT AND THINKER. Mabel Collins.
Dublin University Magazine, November, vol. 90, pp. 610–621.

REVIEW OF PAGE'S THOREAU, HIS LIFE AND AIMS.
Athenæum, November 3.

REVIEW OF PAGE'S THOREAU, HIS LIFE AND AIMS. Thomas
Hughes.
Academy, November 17, vol. 12, pp. 462, 463.
    Reprinted in *Eclectic Magazine*, January, 1878, vol. 90, pp. 114–116.

1878

THOREAU AND NEW ENGLAND TRANSCENDENTALISM.
J. V. O'Connor.
Catholic World, June, vol. 27, pp. 289–300.

1879

HENRY THOREAU. Robert Collyer.
Unity, August 1.
    Reprinted in *Christian Register*, August 16, 1879.

1880

THOREAU [poem]. Muriel Wilton.
Golden Rule, April 14.
Reprinted in *Concord Freeman*, Thoreau Annex, 1880.

HENRY D. THOREAU, SOME RECOLLECTIONS AND INCI-
DENTS CONCERNING HIM, WITH SELECTIONS FROM HIS
WORKS. Joseph Hosmer.
Concord Freeman, Thoreau Annex, [no date].
With cut of Thoreau from Rowse crayon and cut of the
Walden hut and surroundings.

HENRY DAVID THOREAU: HIS CHARACTER AND OPIN-
IONS. R. L. S[tevenson].
Cornhill Magazine, June, vol. 41, pp. 665–682.
Reprinted in *Littell's Living Age*, July 17, 1880, vol. 146,
pp. 179–190; and in the *Eclectic Magazine*, September, 1880,
vol. 95, pp. 257–270.

THOREAU'S PITY AND HUMOUR. Alex. H. Japp.
Spectator, June 12, vol. 53, pp. 749, 750.
A letter replying to certain strictures made by R. L. Steven-
son in the *Cornhill Magazine*. Reprinted in *Littell's Living
Age*, July 17, vol. 146, pp. 190, 191.

AT THOREAU'S CAIRN, WALDEN WOODS, 1879 [poem].
John Albee.
Journal of Speculative Philosophy, July, vol. 14, p. 338.

THOREAU, THE POET-PHILOSOPHER.
Springfield Republican, August 14.
Report of Mr. H. G. O. Blake's remarks and readings at
the Concord School of Philosophy, August 11, 1880.

MR. ALCOTT ON THOREAU.
Concord Freeman, August 19.

PHILOSOPHY AT CONCORD. — II.
Nation, September 2, vol. 31, pp. 164–166.

A NEW ESTIMATE OF THOREAU. William Sloane Kennedy.
The Penn Monthly, October, vol. 11, pp. 794–808.

1881

THOREAU'S WILDNESS. John Burroughs.
Critic, March 26, vol. 1, pp. 74, 75.

THOREAU'S UNPUBLISHED POETRY. F. B. Sanborn.
Critic, March 26, vol. 1, pp. 75, 76.
With (p. 73) a reproduction of the New Bedford ambrotype
of Thoreau, — the first publication of this portrait.

THOREAU'S PORTRAIT — BY HIMSELF.
Literary World (Boston), March 26, vol. 12, pp. 116, 117.
A review of *Early Spring in Massachusetts*.

HENRY DAVID THOREAU. F. B. Sanborn.
The Harvard Register, April, vol. 3, pp. 214–217.

REVIEW OF EARLY SPRING IN MASSACHUSETTS. Isabella
King.
The Harvard Register, April, vol. 3, pp. 233, 234.

PORTRAITS OF THOREAU WITH A BEARD. W. S. K[ennedy].
Critic, April 9, vol. 1, p. 95.
Takes exception to the editorial statement in the preceding
number of the *Critic* that the ambrotype was the only bearded
portrait of Thoreau, and mentions two others, one the Worcester
daguerreotype of 1856, the other a portrait said to have also
been taken in Worcester, a few years before his death, but now
unknown, unless it is the tintype mentioned below.

THOREAU'S JOURNAL.
Independent, April 14.
A review of *Early Spring in Massachusetts*.

REVIEW OF EARLY SPRING.
Yale Literary Magazine, May, vol. 46, pp. 353, 354.

1882

HENRY D. THOREAU. John Burroughs.
Century Magazine, July, vol. 2, pp. 368–379.
Heading the article is a woodcut of Thoreau, which the motto
describes as "from his last portrait, a tintype, taken by Critcher-
son, of Worcester, Mass., in 1861." The original of the cut is

very evidently one of the daguerreotypes taken by Maxham of Worcester in 1856, which were *not* his last portraits, and the tintype must have been taken from the daguerreotype, not directly from the sitter.

SANBORN'S THOREAU. [A. G. Sedgwick.]
Nation, July 13, vol. 35, pp. 34, 35.

REVIEW OF SANBORN'S LIFE OF THOREAU. T. A. J[anvier].
American, July 15, vol. 4, p. 218.

CONCORD AND THOREAU.
Literary World (Boston), July 15, vol. 13, pp. 227, 228.
A review of Sanborn's Life of Thoreau.

REMINISCENCES OF EMERSON. John Albee.
New York Daily Tribune, Sunday, July 23.
A paper read July 22 at the Concord School of Philosophy. Contains an account of a day with Emerson and Thoreau. Reprinted in *Concord Lectures on Philosophy*, 1883.

THOREAU [Review of Sanborn's Life]. H. N. Powers.
Dial (Chicago), August, vol. 3, pp. 70, 71.

REVIEW OF SANBORN'S LIFE OF THOREAU. [George William Curtis.]
Harper's Monthly, September, vol. 65, pp. 631, 632.

SOME RECOLLECTIONS OF RALPH WALDO EMERSON. Edwin P. Whipple.
Harper's Monthly, September, vol. 65, pp. 576-587.
Matter relating to Thoreau on pp. 581, 582.

REVIEW OF SANBORN'S LIFE OF THOREAU. James Purves.
Academy, October 14, vol. 22, pp. 271, 272.

REVIEW OF EARLY SPRING IN MASSACHUSETTS AND SANBORN'S LIFE OF THOREAU. [Theodore Watts.]
Athenæum, October 28, vol. 2 of 1882, pp. 558-560.

1883

HENRY THOREAU'S MOTHER. E. M. F. [Mrs. Jean Munroe Le Brun.]
Boston Daily Advertiser, February 14.
Reprinted in *Concord Freeman*, February 23.

THOREAU'S EXAMPLE.
Spectator, February 17, vol. 56, pp. 239, 240.
A review of Sanborn's Life of Thoreau.

1884

THOREAU'S "SUMMER." Sara A. Underwood.
The Index, June 26, vol. 4 (N. S.), p. 615.

THOREAU IN SUMMER.
Literary World (Boston), July 12, vol. 15, p. 223.
A review of *Summer*.

REVIEW OF SUMMER.
Nation, July 31, vol. 39, pp. 98, 99.

EMERSON AND THE CONCORD SCHOOL OF PHILOSOPHY.
F. M. Holland.
The Index, August 7, vol. 5 (N. S.), pp. 63, 64.

REVIEW OF SUMMER. Walter Lewin.
Academy, September 27, vol. 26, pp. 193, 194.

1885

THOREAU. [A. H. Japp.]
Spectator, January 24, vol. 58, pp. 122, 123.
A review of *Walden* and *Summer*.

"THE DIAL": AN HISTORICAL AND BIOGRAPHICAL IN-
TRODUCTION, WITH A LIST OF THE CONTRIBUTORS.
George Willis Cooke.
Journal of Speculative Philosophy, July, vol. 19, pp. 225–265.
Thoreau matter on pp. 242, 243. Corrigenda on pp. 322, 323
of the same number.

CONCORD MEN AND MEMORIES. George B. Bartlett.
Bay State Monthly, September, vol. 3, pp. 224–232.

[REPORT OF THE CONCORD 250TH ANNIVERSARY CELE-
BRATION. Address by James Russell Lowell.]
Concord Transcript, September 19.
"And I think that we are indebted to Mr. Thoreau, the third

of the three, for another lesson, almost as important; and that
is, that Nature is as friendly, as inspiring, here as in Words-
worth's country, or anywhere else."

1886

THE POETRY OF THOREAU. Joel Benton.
Lippincott's Monthly Magazine, May, vol. 37, pp. 491–500.

HENRY D. THOREAU. H. S. Salt.
Temple Bar, November, vol. 78, pp. 369–383.
    Reprinted in *Eclectic Magazine*, January, 1887, vol. 108,
pp. 89–98; *Library Magazine*, December 18, 1886, vol. 2, pp.
174–181; and *Critic*, November 26 and December 3, 1887,
vol. 11, pp. 276–278, 289–291.

1887

HENRY DAVID THOREAU. A. H. Japp.
Welcome, November, vol. 14, pp. 652–656.
    With woodcut of the Ricketson medallion.

1888

THOREAU'S WINTER JOURNAL.
Literary World (Boston), January 7, vol. 19, p. 4.

SUNDAY AT CONCORD. Grant Allen.
Fortnightly Review, May, vol. 49, pp. 675–690.

HENRY DAVID THOREAU. Francis H. Underwood.
Good Words, July, vol. 29, pp. 445–452.

1889

HENRY DAVID THOREAU. John Burroughs.
Chautauquan, June, vol. 9, pp. 530–533.

A WEEK ON THE CONCORD.
Saturday Review, August 17, vol. 68, pp. 195, 196.

1890

THOREAU: A GLIMPSE. S. A. Jones.
Unitarian, January, February, March, vol. 5, pp. 18–20, 65–
68, 124–128.

HENRY DAVID THOREAU.
London Evening Post, January 10.

EMERSON'S TALKS WITH A COLLEGE BOY. Charles J. Woodbury.
Century Magazine, February, vol. 17, pp. 621–627.

THOREAU'S POETRY. H. S. Salt.
Art Review (London), May, vol. 1, pp. 153–155.

THOREAU'S "ANTI-SLAVERY AND REFORM PAPERS." H. S. Salt.
Lippincott's Magazine, English Edition, August, pp. 277–283.

IN THOREAU'S COUNTRY. A. L.
New York Evening Post, Weekly, October 10.

THE LIFE OF THOREAU.
London Standard, October 16.

THOREAU'S LIFE. [A. H. Japp.]
Spectator, October 18, vol. 65, pp. 526–528.
A review of Salt's Life of Thoreau.

REVIEW OF SALT'S LIFE OF THOREAU, AND OF ANTI-SLAVERY AND REFORM PAPERS, EDITED BY H. S. SALT. Walter Lewin.
Academy, October 25, vol. 38, pp. 357, 358.

THOREAU.
Speaker, November 8, vol. 2, pp. 529, 530.
A review of Salt's Life and his edition of the *Anti-Slavery and Reform Papers*.

THE LIFE OF THOREAU. W. H. Dircks.
Newcastle (England) *Daily Leader*, November 25.

LIFE OF H. D. THOREAU.
Animal World (London), December.

EMERSON AND HIS FRIENDS IN CONCORD. Frank B. Sanborn.
New England Magazine, December, new series, vol. 3, pp. 413–431. Illustrated.

THOREAU. J. L. Otter.
Nature Notes: The Selborne Society's Magazine, December
15, vol. 1, pp. 185–188.

1891

THOREAU'S GOSPEL OF SIMPLICITY. H. S. Salt.
Paternoster Review, March.

AN AFTERNOON IN THE UNIVERSITY LIBRARY. [Samuel
A. Jones.]
The Inlander (Ann Arbor, Mich.), June, vol. 1, pp. 150–153.

THOREAU AND HIS BIOGRAPHERS. Samuel Arthur Jones.
Lippincott's Monthly Magazine, August, vol. 48, pp. 224–228.

TEN VOLUMES OF THOREAU. Joshua W. Caldwell.
New Englander, November, vol. 55, pp. 404–424.

JAMES RUSSELL LOWELL. S. A. J[ones].
The Inlander (Ann Arbor, Mich.), December, vol. 2, pp. 121–
125.

GLIMPSES OF AUTHORS. IV. THE TRANSCENDENTAL
AUTHORS. Thomas Wentworth Higginson.
Brains (Boston), December 1, vol. 1, pp. 103–106.
Gives an amusing account of a lecture delivered by Thoreau
in Boston at Higginson's request and risk.

1892

[ON SOME OF THOREAU'S POEMS.] F. B. Sanborn.
Boston Daily Advertiser, March 8.
In the "Breakfast Table" column.

[ON THOREAU'S READING.] F. B. Sanborn.
Boston Daily Advertiser, March 18.
In the "Breakfast Table" column.

HENRY D. THOREAU'S WORKS.
The Truth Seeker (New York), March 26.

A FAITHFUL LOVER OF NATURE. W. I. Lincoln Adams.
Frank Leslie's Popular Monthly, May, vol. 33, pp. 574–576.
With a woodcut after the daguerreotype.

THE EMERSON-THOREAU CORRESPONDENCE. F. B. Sanborn.
Atlantic Monthly, May, June, vol. 69, pp. 577–596, 736–753.

REVIEW OF AUTUMN. F. B. Sanborn.
Boston Daily Advertiser, September 14.
In "The Breakfast Table."

REVIEW OF AUTUMN. J. B. P.
Vassar Miscellany, November, vol. 22, pp. 92–94.

1893

THOREAU'S INHERITANCE. S. A. Jones.
The Inlander (Ann Arbor, Mich.), February, vol. 3, pp. 199–204.

REMINISCENCES OF THOREAU. Crayon [Horace R. Hosmer].
Concord Enterprise, April 13 and 20.

FAMOUS OLD LANDMARK.
Boston Globe, May 16.
Of the house at 57 Prince St., Boston, then about to be torn down. This house was occupied at one time by John Thoreau, grandfather of H. D. Thoreau. A good cut of the house is printed.

REVIEW OF SANBORN'S LIFE.
The Truth Seeker, June 24.

AN IDEAL FOR FREETHINKERS. [E. M. McDonald.]
The Truth Seeker, June 24.

THOREAU.
Belgravia, August, vol. 81, pp. 375–383.

THOREAU AND HIS ENGLISH FRIEND THOMAS CHOLMONDELEY. F. B. Sanborn.
Atlantic Monthly, December, vol. 72, pp. 741–756.

THOREAU. John Trevor.
Labour Prophet, December, vol. 2, p. 190.

THE RIVERSIDE THOREAU [Review].
Boston Herald, December 18.

THOREAU: LOVE OF NATURE. Edward A. Horton.
Noble Lives and Noble Deeds: A Series of Lessons for Sunday Schools, No. 36.

1894

THOREAU AND HIS WORKS. S. A. Jones.
The Inlander (Ann Arbor, Mich.), vol. 4, pp. 234–240.
A review of the Riverside Edition.

OF THE THOREAUS. Irving Allen.
Boston Daily Advertiser, April 23.

MR. SANBORN CORRECTS MR. ALLEN.
Boston Daily Advertiser, April 25.

MR. ALLEN'S RETORT COURTEOUS.
Boston Daily Advertiser, May 3.

THE THOREAUS. E. J. Loomis.
Boston Daily Advertiser, May 8.

MY FIRST VISIT TO NEW ENGLAND, FOURTH PART.
William Dean Howells.
Harper's Monthly, August, vol. 89, pp. 441–451.
Matter relating to Thoreau on pp. 444, 446–448.

THOREAU'S LETTERS [Review of *Familiar Letters*]. Louis
J. Block.
Dial (Chicago), October 16, vol. 17, pp. 228–230.

HENRY DAVID THOREAU. George Stewart.
Canadian Magazine, December, vol. 4, pp. 101–109.

1895

THOREAU. W. J. Jupp.
Great Thoughts, January 19 and 26, pp. 256–258, 268, 287.

THOREAU'S POEMS OF NATURE. F. B. Sanborn.
Scribner's Magazine, March, vol. 17, pp. 352–355.
Contains a few of Thoreau's poems and also a letter to Emerson dated March 11, 1842, which apparently has not otherwise been published.

REVIEW OF SALT'S SELECTIONS FROM THOREAU. Walter Lewin.
Academy, May 4, vol. 47, p. 377.

THOREAU. Charles C. Abbott.
Lippincott's Monthly Magazine, June, vol. 55, pp. 852–855.

A VISIT TO WALDEN POND. Hector Waylen.
Natural Food, July, pp. 438, 439.

ANENT THOREAU. Alfred W. Hosmer.
Natural Food, September.
A letter correcting certain errors in Mr. Waylen's article.

AMERICAN WOMEN TO WHOM THE WORLD IS INDEBTED. Irving Allen.
The Independent, July 25, vol. 47, pp. 987, 988.
A column about Thoreau's mother and his sister Sophia.

HENRY DAVID THOREAU. I. R. W. [Ina Russelle Warren].
The Magazine of Poetry (Buffalo, N. Y.), October, vol. 7, p. 421.

A DAY AFIELD. Kate Tryon.
Boston Daily Advertiser, October 15.

A THOREAU GROUP.
Boston Daily Advertiser, October 26.

REMINISCENCES OF THOREAU.
Boston Globe, October 26.

AN EVENING WITH THOREAU. [Alfred W. Hosmer.]
High School Voice (Concord, Mass.).
The last three articles are reports of a gathering at Concord, Mass., where Thoreau was discussed and reminiscences of him were exchanged. Among the speakers were George B. Bartlett, Walton Ricketson, Miss Jane Hosmer, and Alfred W. Hosmer.

THOREAU AS A POET.
London Daily Chronicle, November 9.
Review of *Poems of Nature*.

CONCORD: AND THOSE WHO HAVE MADE IT FAMOUS. H. Hayes Robbins.
The Unitarian, December, vol. 10, pp. 538–543.

CONCORD LETTER. K. L. E. [Kate L. Edwards].
Southbridge (Mass.) *Journal*, December 5.

"TRANSCENDENTAL WILD OATS." Annie J. Ward.
Springfield Republican, December 15.
Letters of Mrs. A. B. Alcott with references to Mrs. Thoreau.

OF HIGH PLACES ABOUT THE HISTORIC TOWN OF CONCORD. Kate Tryon.
Boston Daily Advertiser, December 18.

1896

AN EVENING WITH THOREAU. Alfred W. Hosmer.
Seed-Time (London), January.
Report of the Concord gathering of October, 1895.

THOREAU'S VERSES.
Saturday Review, January 18, vol. 81, p. 55.
A review of *Poems of Nature*.

REVIEW OF POEMS OF NATURE. Richard Le Gallienne.
London Star, January 23.

THOREAU'S UNCLE PETER. M. B. Wright.
Boston Transcript, February 8.

THOREAU'S VOICE. S. E. Rena.
Boston Transcript, February 15.

AMONG THE AUTHORS: HENRY DAVID THOREAU. Henry S. Salt.
Vegetarian Review (London), May, pp. 225–228.

THOREAU AND THE WALDEN WOODS. F. B. Sanborn.
Boston Herald, May 26.

THOREAU. S. F. W.
Inquirer (London), July 18.
Review of Salt's Life.

THE GREENACRE SCHOOL: EMERSON DAY.
Boston Transcript, August 15.
Report of an address by F. B. Sanborn.

THOREAU'S CONCORD. Philip G. Hubert, Jr.
New York Tribune, September 13.
Reprinted in *Boston Herald*, September 30, 1896.

"LIFE OF HENRY DAVID THOREAU."
Critic, September 19, vol. 29, p. 172.
Review of Salt's Life.

THOREAU AS A PROSE WRITER. Hiram M. Stanley.
Dial (Chicago), October 1, vol. 21, pp. 179–182.

REVIEW OF POEMS OF NATURE.
Athenæum, October 17, pp. 517, 518.

HENRY DAVID THOREAU.
Literary World (Boston), October 17, vol. 27, pp. 342, 343.
Review of Salt's Life.

EARLY WORCESTER LITERARY DAYS.
Worcester Telegram, October 26.

LOOKING BACK 50 YEARS. H.
Worcester Telegram.
A letter referring to the former article.

LITERARY LANDMARKS OF CONCORD.
Romance, November.

THOREAU. Bradford Torrey.
Atlantic Monthly, December, vol. 78, pp. 822–832.

THOREAU, NEWCOMB, BROOK FARM. [F. B. Sanborn.]
Springfield Republican, December 2.

THE TWO THOREAUS. George W. Cooke.
Independent, December 10, vol. 48, pp. 1671, 1672.

THOREAU'S "CAPE COD" IN COLORS.
Critic, December 19, vol. 29, p. 402.

[REMARKS ON THOREAU AND CAPE COD.]
Boston Transcript, December 19.
In "The Listener."

"THE TWO THOREAUS." F. B. Sanborn.
Independent, December 31, vol. 48, p. 1789.

1897

MEMORIALS OF AMERICAN AUTHORS. Joseph Edgar
Chamberlin.
Atlantic, January, vol. 79, pp. 64–72.
  Matter relating to Thoreau on pp. 68, 69.

THOREAU'S UNPAID OCCUPATIONS. Olivia Thide.
The Bachelor of Arts (New York), February, vol. 4, pp. 65–70.

THOREAU'S HILL. Kate Tryon.
Boston Daily Advertiser, March 23.

THOREAU AND EMERSON. F. B. Sanborn.
Forum, April, vol. 23, pp. 218–227.

AT THOREAU'S POND. Philip G. Hubert, Jr.
Book Buyer, July, vol. 14, pp. 549–557. With illustrations.

JOHN BURROUGHS. Hamilton Wright Mabie.
Century, August, vol. 32, pp. 560–568.

THE GREENACRE LECTURES. A REUNION OF THE
CONCORD SCHOOL OF PHILOSOPHY.
Boston Transcript, August 14.
  Contains a report of an address by F. B. Sanborn on "Walks
and Talks with Emerson and Thoreau."

AMERICAN BOOKMEN. VIII. EMERSON AND CONCORD.
M. A. De Wolfe Howe.
Bookman, November, vol. 6, pp. 203–213.

HENRY D. THOREAU.
The Truth Seeker, November 20.

MEMORIES OF THOREAU. UNPUBLISHED ANECDOTES OF
NEW ENGLAND'S ANTI-PURITAN AUTHOR AND NAT-
URALIST.
The Truth Seeker, November 20.

MEMORIES OF THOREAU, RECALLED BY RALPH WALDO
EMERSON'S SON.
Brooklyn Daily Eagle, November 30.
  Report of a lecture before the Brooklyn Institute by Dr.
Edward W. Emerson.

THE IDEALISTIC BASIS OF THOREAU'S GENIUS. Daniel Gregory Mason.
Harvard Monthly, December, vol. 25, pp. 82–93.

BETWEEN BOOKS. Jennette Barbour Perry.
Boston Transcript, December 1.

HENRY HEINE AND HENRY THOREAU. [F. B. Sanborn.]
Springfield Republican, December 22.

1898

WALDEN [poem].
Boston Transcript, February 26.

"VOX CLAMANTIS IN DESERTO." S. A. J[ones].
The Inlander (Ann Arbor, Mich.), March, vol. 8, pp. 222–230.
Review of the Holiday Edition of *Walden*.

A BOY SIXTY YEARS AGO. George Frisbie Hoar.
Youth's Companion, March 24. (Reprinted in *A Boy Sixty Years Ago* and *Autobiography of Seventy Years*.)

THOREAU'S FRIEND: DEATH OF HARRISON GRAY OTIS BLAKE.
Worcester Evening Gazette, April 19.

[REMINISCENCES OF THOREAU AND OTHERS IN WORCESTER.]
Worcester Evening Gazette, April 21.

THE THOREAU JOURNAL GOES TO E. HARLOW RUSSELL, LITERARY EXECUTOR.
Worcester Evening Gazette, April 25.
Report of the filing of Mr. Blake's will.

HARRISON G. O. BLAKE, '35, AND THOREAU. Daniel Gregory Mason.
Harvard Monthly, May, vol. 26, pp. 87–95.

THE FIRST BOOKS OF SOME AMERICAN AUTHORS. L. S. Livingston.
Bookman (N. Y.), September, vol. 8, pp. 38–43.
The Thoreau matter occupies half a page, and is accompanied by a facsimile of the title-page of the first edition of the *Week*.

THOREAU ILLUSTRATED. H. S. S[alt].
Saturday Review, November 5, vol. 86, pp. 600, 601.

ANOTHER PIONEER GONE. [E. M. Macdonald.]
The Truth Seeker, November 19.
Obituary of Calvin Harlow Greene.

THOREAU'S INCARCERATION (AS TOLD BY HIS JAILER).
S. A. J[ones].
The Inlander (Ann Arbor, Mich.), December, vol. 9, pp. 96–103.

1899

MUSIC AND TRANSCENDENTALISM [CONTAINING A NOTICE OF SOME UNPUBLISHED LETTERS OF HENRY D. AND SOPHIA E. THOREAU]. [F. B. Sanborn.]
Springfield Republican, January 25.

WRITERS THAT ARE QUOTABLE. Bradford Torrey.
Atlantic Monthly, March, vol. 83, pp. 407–411.

FROUDE TO THOREAU. Henry S. Salt.
Academy, March 11, vol. 56, pp. 305, 306.
Review of Jones's *Some Unpublished Letters of Henry D. and Sophia E. Thoreau.*

THOREAU AND HIS TEACHING. K. M. W.
Inquirer (London), September 23 and 30, pp. 603, 604, 619, 620.

THOREAU'S ATTITUDE TOWARD NATURE. Bradford Torrey.
Atlantic Monthly, November, vol. 84, pp. 706–710.

REMINISCENCES OF THOREAU.
Outlook (New York), December 2, vol. 63, pp. 815–821.
"The author of this article, who prefers to leave it unsigned, was an intimate personal friend of the late Miss Sophia E. Thoreau, the sister of Henry D. Thoreau. The two friends often visited each other. Their acquaintance and friendship began when Miss Thoreau was thirty-two years of age, and continued unbroken until her death in 1876. The author of the article during this period made frequent visits to the Thoreau home in Concord, none of them very brief, and many of several

weeks' duration, and participated with absolute freedom in the family life." — Editor's Note.

[ADDRESS ON "HENRY D. THOREAU: THE MAN AND HIS WORK."] [E. Harlow Russell.]
Leominster [Mass.] *Daily Enterprise*, December 28.
Report of an address at a meeting of the Unitarian Club.

1900

LITERATURE OF FIELD AND HEDGEROW.
Nature Notes (London), January, vol. 11, pp. 5–11.

THOREAU AND JEFFERIES. Henry S. Salt.
Nature Notes, February, vol. 11, pp. 22, 23.

THOREAU AS A HUMORIST. George Beardsley.
Dial (Chicago), April 1, vol. 28, pp. 241–243.

THOREAU'S PHILOSOPHY OF LIFE. Louis René Kaufman.
Columbia Literary Monthly, May, vol. 8, pp. 241–247.

THOREAU. Frederick M. Smith.
Critic, July, vol. 37, pp. 60–67.

THOREAU AND GILBERT WHITE. Henry S. Salt.
New Age (London), November 15.

1901

UNPUBLISHED LETTERS OF THOREAU.
New York Times, March 9.
Review of Jones's *Some Unpublished Letters of Henry D. and Sophia E. Thoreau.*

THE GOSPEL OF THE OPEN: HENRY D. THOREAU. Ella Gilbert Ives.
Boston Transcript, April 24.

PERTAINING TO THOREAU.
New York Times Saturday Review, May 25.
Review of Dr. Jones's book of that name.

A HERMIT'S NOTES ON THOREAU. Paul Elmer More.
Atlantic Monthly, June, vol. 87, pp. 857–864.

THOREAU AND HIS CRITICS. W. M. [Wilhelm Miller].
Country Life in America, November, vol. 1, pp. xiv–xvi.
Review of *Pertaining to Thoreau*.

ABOUT LOWELL AND THOREAU. [F. B. Sanborn.]
Springfield Republican, December 11.

THOREAU'S PERSONALITY. George H. Sargent.
Boston Transcript, December 14.
Review of *The Personality of Thoreau*.

1902

THOREAU: HIS PERSONALITY AS MR. SANBORN REMEM-
BERS IT.
New York Times, January 11.

THOREAU. T. M. P.
New Age (London), January 16.
Review of "H. A. Page's" Life.

THE CARLISLE PINES. E. H. B[riggs].
Middlesex Patriot (Concord, Mass.), January 24.

IMMORTALITY OF PINES. E. H. B[riggs].
Ditto, February 14.

THOREAU AND THE PINES. James B. Wood.
Ditto, February 21.
Contains reminiscences of Thoreau.

THE LATE WILLIAM ELLERY CHANNING. Annie Russell
Marble.
Critic, February, vol. 40, pp. 114, 115.

REVIEW OF SANBORN'S THE PERSONALITY OF THOREAU.
Nation, February 6, vol. 74, p. 114.

ELLERY CHANNING IN NEW HAMPSHIRE. F. B. Sanborn.
Granite Monthly, March, vol. 32, pp. 157–164.

THOREAU. S. E. Saville.
Gentleman's Magazine, April, new series, vol. 68, pp. 400–409.

THOREAU'S LUXURY. F. M. Holland.
Boston Investigator, April 26.

NOTICE OF THE SERVICE.
New York Evening Post, May 16.

REVIEW OF THE SERVICE.
Boston Transcript, May 21.

A NOTABLE NEW BOOK. S. A. Jones.
Detroit Journal, May 22.
Review of *The Service*.

AN UNPUBLISHED ESSAY BY THOREAU.
New York Times Saturday Review, May 31.
Review of *The Service*.

WHERE THOREAU WORKED AND WANDERED. Annie
Russell Marble.
Critic, June, vol. 40, pp. 509–516.
Illustrated. The illustrations include a half-tone reproduction
of two pages of Thoreau's manuscript journal.

THOREAU. Hugh de Selincourt.
Oxford Point of View, June, pp. 91–98.

WALKS WITH ELLERY CHANNING. [Selections from Emer-
son's Journal, edited by T. W. Higginson.]
Atlantic Monthly, July, vol. 90, pp. 27–34.
Thoreau matter on pp. 29–33.

THOREAU [sonnet]. James Buckham.
Munsey's Magazine, July, vol. 27, pp. 604, 605.

EMERSON, THOREAU, CHANNING. [F. B. Sanborn.]
Springfield Republican, July 2.
On the Channing article in the July *Atlantic*.

REVIEW OF THE SERVICE.
Nation, August 7, vol. 75, pp. 117, 118.

UN POÈTE-NATURALISTE AMÉRICAIN: HENRY DAVID THO-
REAU. Maurice Muret.
La Revue, August 15 and September 1, vol. 42, pp. 428–436,
572–580.

A Bit of Unpublished Correspondence between Henry Thoreau and Isaac Hecker. E. H. Russell.
Atlantic Monthly, September, vol. 90, pp. 370–376.

German and American Writers. [F. B. Sanborn.]
Springfield Republican, September 3.
Of Thoreau and Schiller, of Channing's Life of Thoreau, and other matters pertaining to Thoreau.

Two Famous Bachelors and their Love-Stories. Clara Laughlin.
Book Buyer, October, vol. 25, pp. 241–247.
Of the love-stories of Thoreau and Washington Irving.

Biography and Criticism. [F. B. Sanborn.]
Springfield Republican, October 15.

Thoreau the Poet-Naturalist.
Boston Transcript, November 12.
Review of Sanborn's edition of Channing's book.

Review of Mrs. Marble's Thoreau: His Home, Friends, and Books.
Nation, November 13, vol. 75, p. 388.

Review of Sanborn's Edition of Channing's Life.
Nation, November 20, vol. 75, p. 403.

A Thanksgiving Pilgrimage to Thoreau. D. G. M. [Daniel Gregory Mason].
Boston Transcript, November 26.

Recent Estimates of Thoreau.
Literary Digest, November 29, vol. 25, p. 706.

Review of Mrs. Marble's Thoreau.
Critic, December, vol. 41, pp. 512, 513.

Thoreau.
Independent, December 11, vol. 54, pp. 2959–2960.
A review of Sanborn's edition of Channing's Life and Mrs. Marble's *Thoreau*.

AN OLD AND A NEW ESTIMATE OF THOREAU. Edith Kellogg Dunton.
Dial (Chicago), December 16, vol. 33, pp. 464–466.
A review of Sanborn's edition of Channing's *Thoreau, the Poet-Naturalist*, and Mrs. Marble's *Thoreau: His Home, Friends, and Books*.

1903

THOREAU. T. [Horace Traubel].
The Conservator (Philadelphia), January, 13th year, p. 171.
Review of Sanborn's edition of Channing's Life.

[REVIEW OF SANBORN'S EDITION OF CHANNING'S THO-REAU.]
Athenæum, January 17.

CONCORD'S FAMOUS SON. Henry Waterman.
Boston Home Journal, January 17.

CHANNING'S LIFE OF THOREAU. John Albee.
Springfield Republican, February 1.
Review of Sanborn's edition.

COOKE'S BOOK ON EMERSON'S DIAL. [F. B. Sanborn.]
Springfield Republican, February 15.

BOOKS ABOUT NATURE. Henry Childs Merwin.
Scribner's Magazine, April, vol. 33, pp. 430–437.

THOREAU [quatrain]. Charlotte Becker.
New England Magazine, May, vol. 28, p. 376.

ESQUISSE D'UNE PHILOSOPHIE DES CONVENTIONS SO-CIALES. Albert Schinz.
Revue Philosophique de la France et de l'Etranger, June, vol. 55, pp. 601–633.
Largely a criticism of Thoreau's philosophy.

WAS THOREAU A LOVER OF NATURE? Jennette Barbour Perry.
Critic, August, vol. 43, p. 152.

HENRY DAVID THOREAU: AND THE HUMANE STUDY OF
NATURAL HISTORY. [Henry S. Salt.]
The Humane Review (London), October, pp. 220–229.

HENRY THOREAU — AN ESTIMATE. Walter Leighton.
Arena, November, vol. 30, pp. 489–498.

1904

COUNTRY HOMES OF FAMOUS AMERICANS. IV. HENRY
DAVID THOREAU. Oliver Bronson Capen.
Country Life in America, February, vol. 5, pp. 285–288. Illustrated.
Reprinted in *Country Homes of Famous Americans*, Doubleday, Page & Co., 1905.

THE DEATH OF THOREAU'S GUIDE. Fannie Hardy Eckstorm.
Atlantic Monthly, June, vol. 93, pp. 736–746.
Some account of the life and death of Joseph Attien, an
Indian river-driver, who served as guide to Thoreau on his
Chesuncook excursion.

[REMARKS ON THOREAU AND JOHN MUIR.] Francis H.
Allen.
Boston Transcript, July 13.
In "The Observer."

1905

THOREAU AS A DIARIST. Bradford Torrey.
Atlantic Monthly, January, vol. 95, pp. 5–18.

HENRY DAVID THOREAU. Will D. Howe.
The Reader Magazine, February, vol. 5, pp. 372–376.

ON BALLS OF VEGETABLE MATTER FROM SANDY SHORES.
W. F. Ganong.
Rhodora (Boston), March, vol. 7, pp. 41–47.
Reference to the balls found by Thoreau at Flint's Pond on
pp. 41, 42.

THOREAU, A PROPHET OF NATURE. Hamilton W. Mabie.
Outlook, June 3, vol. 80, pp. 278–282.

THOREAU [poem]. Florence Kiper.
New England Magazine, August, vol. 32, p. 656.
Reprinted in *Current Literature*, October, 1905, vol. 39, p. 458.

A CONCORD NOTE-BOOK: ELLERY CHANNING AND HIS
TABLE-TALK. THIRD PAPER. F. B. Sanborn.
Critic, September, vol. 47, pp. 267–272.

THOREAU AND ELLERY CHANNING. F. B. Sanborn.
Critic, November, vol. 47, pp. 444–451.
The Fifth Paper of "A Concord Note-Book."

THE DIARY OF A POET-NATURALIST.
Current Literature, November, vol. 39, pp. 510–512.
A review of Thoreau's Journal as published in part in the
Atlantic, and of Mr. Torrey's "Thoreau as a Diarist."

1906

In A CONCORD NOTE-BOOK: THE WOMEN OF CONCORD.
F. B. Sanborn.
Critic, February, March, April, May, vol. 48, pp. 157, 158,
254–257, 343–346, 410–413.

[ON THOREAU AND FIREPLACES.]
Mount Tom: An All Outdoors Magazine, edited by Gerald
Stanley Lee, Northampton, Mass., March, vol. 1, pp. 334–
337.

THOREAU AND HIS CRITICS. Gilbert P. Coleman.
Dial (Chicago), June 1, vol. 40, pp. 352–356.

AFTER READING THOREAU [poem]. Emma Bell Miles.
Century, October, vol. 72, p. 855.

MR. TORREY'S THOREAU. H. W. Boynton.
New York Times, October 20.
A review of the first ten volumes of the Walden Edition.

REVIEW OF JOURNAL. P. E. M. [Paul Elmer More].
[New York] Evening Post, November 3 and 10.

LETTER ON ABOVE REVIEW. Francis H. Allen.
[New York] Evening Post, November 17.

THOREAU AND GERMAN ROMANTICISM. P. E. M. [Paul Elmer More].

Nation, November 8 and 15, vol. 83, pp. 388–390, 411, 412.

The review of the *Journal* appearing in the *Evening Post,* November 3 and 10.

1907

THOREAU AND THE SIMPLE LIFE. Henry S. Salt.

Humane Review (London), January, pp. 202–208.

A review of the Walden Edition.

NOTICE OF THE LAST TEN VOLUMES OF THE WALDEN EDITION.

New York Evening Post, January 15.

NOTICE OF THE LAST TEN VOLUMES OF THE WALDEN EDITION.

Nation, January 17, vol. 84, p. 56.

THE COMPLETE THOREAU.

Chicago Evening Post, January 19.

A review of the Walden Edition.

RALEIGH, THOREAU, AND OTHERS. [F. B. Sanborn.]

Springfield Republican, January 23.

In his regular "Boston Literary Letter" Mr. Sanborn writes of Thoreau's essay on Raleigh, published by the Bibliophile Society; of the Walden Edition of Thoreau's Writings; and of *The First and Last Journeys of Thoreau,* also issued by the Bibliophile Society.

THOREAU IN HIS JOURNALS. F. B. Sanborn.

Dial (Chicago), February 16, vol. 42, pp. 107–110.

A review of the Walden edition.

NOTICE OF WALDEN EDITION.

Litterarisches Echo (Berlin), March 15.

THOREAU'S BRIGHT WORLD.

Boston Transcript, March 16.

A review of the Walden Edition of Thoreau's Writings.

THE DIARY OF THOREAU.
Haverhill Evening Gazette, March 28.
Concerning Thoreau's visits to Haverhill as recorded in the *Journal*.

THE MAN WHO WAS ALWAYS A BOY. Gilbert P. Coleman.
St. Nicholas, May, vol. 34, pp. 617–622.

THOREAU'S WORKS IN NEW EDITION.
New York Times, July 6.
Review of the last ten volumes of the Walden Edition.

REVIEW OF FINAL TEN VOLUMES OF THE WALDEN EDITION. T. B.
Chicago Evening Post, December 7.

1908

THOREAU IN VERMONT IN 1856. Mrs. Elizabeth B. Davenport.
Vermont Botanical Club, Bulletin No. 3 (Burlington, Vt.), April (Annual), pp. 36–38.
Contains reminiscences of Thoreau's visit in Brattleboro, Vt., in September, 1856, by Mrs. Mary Brown Dunton, of Sheboygan, Wis., in whose father's house, Rev. Addison Brown's, Thoreau stayed; with extracts from three unpublished letters of Thoreau.

THOREAU IN TWENTY VOLUMES. Henry S. Salt.
Fortnightly Review, June, vol. 83, n. s., pp. 994–1004.
Reprinted in *The Living Age*, July 18, 1908, vol. 258, pp. 131–139.

THOREAU'S "MAINE WOODS." Fannie Hardy Eckstorm.
Atlantic, August, vol. 102, pp. 242–250.

AUCTION PRICES

AUCTION PRICES

For this record of the sales of Thoreau's books and manuscripts at auction the reader is indebted to the annual publication "American Book-Prices Current," from which it has been gathered with the permission of the compiler, Mr. Luther S. Livingston. Mr. Livingston has also kindly supplied the information concerning the sales for 1908 in advance of the publication of the volume for the current year. The name of the sale, where given, generally indicates the original owner of the lot, but not invariably, since odd lots are not infrequently sold in connection with the sales of libraries and collections. Where the word "sale" is omitted the name is that of the auctioneer.

Items bringing less than $3.00 are not recorded in "American Book-Prices Current."

AUTUMN, 1892, FIRST EDITION

Arnold sale, January, 1901	$5.00
Bangs, October, 1901	4.12
Bangs, November, 1902	3.75
Somerby sale, December, 1903	3.00
Anderson, November, 1904	3.20
Anderson, April, 1905	3.25
Anderson, January, 1906	8.00
Pyser sale, February, 1906	6.00
Merwin-Clayton, February, 1906	5.25
Merwin-Clayton, March, 1906	4.00
Merwin-Clayton, May, 1906	4.50
Merwin-Clayton, November, 1906	4.00
Anderson, October, 1907	3.00
Merwin-Clayton, January, 1908	3.00

BIT OF UNPUBLISHED CORRESPONDENCE BETWEEN HENRY D. THOREAU AND ISAAC T. HECKER, 1902

Greene sale, October, 1903; uncut	$3.25

CAPE COD, 1865, FIRST EDITION

Roos sale, April, 1897	$4.25
Bangs, October, 1900	3.85

Arnold sale, January, 1901 $6.00
Anderson, February, 1901; name written on first page   5.25
Libbie, December, 1901   5.00
May sale, January, 1903   6.25
Bangs, January, 1903   5.50
Brown sale, April, 1903; uncut   3.50
Bartlett sale, May, 1903; uncut   5.50
Reid sale, November, 1903   4.85
Anderson, January, 1904; name on title   3.50
French and Chubbuck sale, February, 1904   5.25
Stephens sale, April, 1904   4.10
Knapp sale, February, 1905   5.50
Libbie, March, 1905   4.12
Drowne sale, December, 1905   5.00
Pattee sale, December, 1905; uncut   3.25
Pyser sale, February, 1906   5.00
Coverly sale, February, 1906; uncut   4.00
Searing sale, February, 1906   5.50
Street sale, May, 1906   4.00
Warner sale, March, 1907   3.25
Drake sale, May, 1907   4.25
Merwin-Clayton, January, 1908   3.75
Williamson sale, January, 1908   4.00

CAPE COD, 2 vols., 1896

Anderson, April, 1905; half morocco, gilt top, uncut $4.00

EARLY SPRING, 1881, FIRST EDITION

Arnold sale, January, 1901 $5.50
Bangs, October, 1901   4.13
Anderson, January, 1906   8.00
Merwin-Clayton, February, 1906   10.00
Brandon sale, February, 1906   4.75
Merwin-Clayton, May, 1906   5.75
Warner sale, March, 1907   4.75
Merwin-Clayton, January, 1908   3.10

EXCURSIONS, 1863, FIRST EDITION

Mackay sale, April, 1900 $3.25
McKee sale, November, 1900   6.50
Arnold sale, January, 1901   8.00
Anderson, February, 1901   3.50

Libbie, December, 1901	$5.00
Cox sale, February, 1902	6.00
Bangs, October, 1902	4.50
Bangs, January, 1903	6.00
Brown sale, April, 1903; uncut	3.50
Bartlett sale, May, 1903	4.50
Anderson, January, 1904	4.50
Anderson, March, 1904	4.00
Stephens sale, April, 1904	5.00
Libbie, June, 1904	4.50
Knapp sale, February, 1905	7.00
Gordon sale, April, 1905	3.50
Alger sale, May, 1905	3.25
Merwin-Clayton, September, 1905	4.00
Drowne sale, December, 1905	6.50
Pattee sale, December, 1905	3.50
Anderson, January, 1906	6.00
Pyser sale, February, 1906	5.00
Searing sale, February, 1906	5.00
Barry sale, May, 1906	4.25
Merwin-Clayton, November, 190′	4.25
Hoppock sale, December, 1906	3.10
Anderson, January, 1907	3.25
Anderson, October, 1907	3.00
Merwin-Clayton, January, 1908	3.50
Williamson sale, January, 1908	3.50
Libbie, April, 1908	3.10
Anderson, May, 1908	3.00
Libbie, May, 1908	3.75

JONES'S BIBLIOGRAPHY

Bangs, February, 1896	$8.25
Williamson sale, January, 1908	8.00

JONES'S PERTAINING TO THOREAU

Merwin-Clayton, May, 1906; uncut	$6.00

LETTERS TO VARIOUS PERSONS, 1865, FIRST EDITION.

Arnold sale, January, 1901	$6.00
Anderson, February, 1901	3.50
Bangs, November, 1901; half levant	4.00
Bangs, April, 1902	3.75

Anderson, May, 1902	$4.75
Lockwood sale, October, 1902	5.25
Libbie, February, 1903	4.00
Peirce sale, May, 1903	5.00
Bartlett sale, May, 1903	4.75
Reid sale, November, 1903	4.35
Anderson, January, 1904	4.85
French and Chubbuck sale, February, 1904	4.50
Anderson, March, 1904	4.15
Knapp sale, February, 1905	4.00
Drowne sale, December, 1905	3.55
Anderson, January, 1906	5.00
Pyser sale, February, 1906	4.00
Merwin-Clayton, February, 1906	4.50
Searing sale, February, 1906	3.50
Williamson sale, January, 1908	1.50
Libbie, June, 1908	6.00

MAINE WOODS, 1864, FIRST EDITION

Avery sale, October, 1900	$3.50
Arnold sale, January, 1901	6.00
Bangs, October, 1902	4.50
Edwards and Scott sale, October, 1902	4.10
May sale, January, 1903; presentation copy to Charles H. Dunbar	17.50
Bangs, January, 1903	5.00
Whipple sale, April, 1903	4.62
Bartlett sale, May, 1903	6.50
O'Shaughnessy sale, November, 1903	4.25
Anderson, January, 1904; name on title	3.20
Conland sale, January, 1904	3.40
French and Chubbuck sale, February, 1904	4.25
Anderson, October, 1904; back faded	3.00
Knapp sale, February, 1905	6.50
Eames sale, May, 1905	4.50
Drowne sale, December, 1905	7.00
Merwin-Clayton, January, 1906	3.00
Anderson, January, 1906	5.50
Pyser sale, February, 1906	7.00
Brandon sale, February, 1906	5.00
Searing sale, February, 1906	5.00

Barry sale, May, 1906	$4.80
Anderson, October, 1906	3.00
Anderson, June, 1907	6.50
Merwin-Clayton, January, 1908	3.75
Williamson sale, January, 1908	3.50

OF FRIENDSHIP, 1901

Conely sale, October, 1902; uncut	$3.25
Bangs, January, 1903; uncut	6.20
Anderson, February, 1903; uncut	9.00
Anderson, December, 1903; uncut	4.00
Anderson, October, 1904	6.00
Bangs sale, November, 1905; uncut	6.00
Drowne sale, December, 1905; uncut	6.00
Merwin-Clayton, February, 1906; uncut	8.00

PEABODY'S (ELIZABETH P.) ÆSTHETIC PAPERS

Arnold sale, January, 1901; paper, uncut	$8.50
Bangs, February, 1901	5.75
Whipple sale, April, 1903; paper, uncut; small nail-hole in front cover and title-page	5.25
Brown sale, April, 1903; paper, uncut	5.00
Libbie, June, 1903; half morocco; a few leaves stained	3.00
Libbie, January, 1904; library stamp on title	4.00

POEMS OF NATURE, 1895, FIRST EDITION

Cobb sale, March, 1906; uncut	$3.50

REDPATH'S ECHOES OF HARPER'S FERRY

Arnold sale, January, 1901	$11.00

SERVICE, THE

Peirce sale, March, 1903; uncut	$3.20
Comstock sale, May, 1906; uncut	3.25
Williamson sale, January, 1908	3.00

SERVICE, THE, *Japan Paper*

May sale, January, 1903; uncut	$11.00
Anderson, February, 1903	7.85
Wales sale, March, 1903; uncut	8.50
Anderson, January, 1904	5.60

SOME UNPUBLISHED LETTERS OF HENRY D. AND SOPHIA E. THOREAU

French sale, April, 1901	$13.00

Bangs, February, 1902; uncut	$4.75
Peirce sale, March, 1903; uncut	6.50
Wales sale, March, 1903; uncut	4.75
Anderson, April, 1903	4.25
Goodwin sale, November, 1903; uncut	3.50
Anderson, March, 1904; uncut	6.00
Pyser sale, February, 1906; uncut	10.00
Merwin-Clayton, May, 1906; uncut	8.50
Merwin-Clayton, May, 1906; uncut	6.25
Williamson sale, January, 1908	6.75

SUMMER, 1884, FIRST EDITION

Bangs, January, 1903	$8.00
Anderson, January, 1904	4.30
Anderson, March, 1904	5.60
Anderson, January, 1906; J. G. Whittier's copy	26.00
Merwin-Clayton, February, 1906	9.50
Brandon sale, February, 1906	5.00
Merwin-Clayton, May, 1906	7.00
Merwin-Clayton, November, 1906	5.20
Merwin-Clayton, January, 1908	3.50

WALDEN, 1854, FIRST EDITION

Bangs, March, 1897; a few passages marked in ink	$4.75
Roos sale, April, 1897	8.00
Bangs, May, 1898	3.13
Carruth sale, May, 1898	4.00
Roos sale, March, 1900	5.25
McKee sale, November, 1900	8.00
Arnold sale, January, 1901	30.00
Bangs, February, 1901; back repaired	4.35
Bangs, May, 1901	25.00
Bangs, October, 1901	10.50
Libbie, December, 1901; presentation copy from the author to H. G. O. Blake with inscription signed with initials; worn	40.00
Bangs, December, 1901	9.25
Libbie, January, 1902	15.50
Bangs, October, 1902	16.00
May sale, January, 1903	15.00
Bangs, January, 1903	14.50
Gilsey sale, March, 1903	10.50

Anderson, May, 1903	$18.00
Bartlett sale, May, 1903	21.00
Reid sale, November, 1903	18.95
Anderson, December, 1903	15.00
Anderson, January, 1904	12.40
French and Chubbuck sale, February, 1904; stamp on title	12.00
Stephens sale, April, 1904	9.00
Libbie, June, 1904	10.50
Anderson, December, 1904	13.00
Anderson, January, 1905	12.00
Knapp sale, February, 1905	16.00
Libbie, March, 1905	13.25
Alger sale, May, 1905; binding stained and name on title	8.00
Hale sale, May, 1905	10.50
Drowne sale, December, 1905	10.00
Anderson, January, 1906	25.25
Pyser sale, February, 1906	18.00
Brandon sale, February, 1906	18.00
Searing sale, February, 1906	19.00
Peacock sale, March, 1906	18.00
Barry sale, May, 1906	14.50
Merwin-Clayton, November, 1906	4.50
Anderson, December, 1906	9.60
Merwin-Clayton, March, 1907	3.25
O'Shaughnessy sale, April, 1907	8.50
Anderson, June, 1907	6.30
Anderson, June, 1907	7.75
Anderson, October, 1907	10.00
Libbie, January, 1908	6.50
Merwin-Clayton, January, 1908	11.00
Williamson sale, January, 1908; advertisements dated April, 1854	14.00
Williamson sale, January, 1908; advertisements dated May, 1854	4.50
Anderson, February, 1908	3.25
Libbie, March, 1908	6.50
Anderson, March, 1908	5.00
Anderson, May, 1908	4.00
Anderson, May, 1908	7.25

WEEK, 1849, FIRST EDITION

Waterbury sale, January, 1895; presentation copy	$7.50
Bangs, March, 1897; presentation copy to Thomas Cholmondeley, with the latter's inscription on fly-leaf	6.25
Roos sale, April, 1897; uncut	14.50
Libbie, January, 1900	5.00
Libbie, April, 1900	27.00
Arnold sale, January, 1901; uncut	52.50
Bangs, November, 1901; half levant	8.50
Libbie, December, 1901; uncut	54.00
Libbie, December, 1901; half calf; presentation copy from the author to H. G. O. Blake, with inscription signed with initials	37.00
Bangs, October, 1902; uncut	48.00
Conely sale, October, 1902; uncut, back badly worn	34.00
May sale, January, 1903; uncut, back worn; presentation copy to Chas. H. Dunbar	77.50
Whipple sale, April, 1903; resewn in original covers	8.00
Anderson, May, 1903; uncut	28.00
Bartlett sale, May, 1903; uncut	35.00
Anderson, January, 1904; uncut; with autograph note in pencil by Thoreau on p. 78	41.00
Anderson, February, 1904; uncut; a little writing on title	17.50
Anderson, March, 1904; uncut	31.00
Anderson, January, 1905; uncut	36.05
Knapp sale, February, 1905; uncut	50.00
Pattee sale, December, 1905; a set of printer's proof sheets, with a correction on p. 117, folded, uncut, in case; corner of one leaf missing	42.00
Pyser sale, February, 1906; uncut	62.00
Merwin-Clayton, February, 1906 [1]	105.00
Searing sale, February, 1906	46.00
Merwin-Clayton, May, 1906	57.50
Tefft sale, November, 1906; uncut	50.00
Anderson, December, 1906; uncut	30.50
O'Shaughnessy sale, April, 1907; uncut	34.00
Anderson, October, 1907	42.00
Williamson sale, January, 1908; with note by F. B.	

[1] The copy sold at the Pattee sale the preceding December.

Sanborn saying that the copy had been bought
from Thoreau himself by Miss Sanborn $60.00
Anderson, March, 1908; presentation copy to Albert
S. Brown, with inscription by Thoreau and with
his correction on p. 396   85.00
Anderson, March, 1908   56.00

WEEK, 1862

Bangs, October, 1901; with library number on top
margin of title $12.00
Drowne sale, December, 1905   10.00
Anderson, January, 1906   12.00
Brandon sale, February, 1906   4.75
Merwin-Clayton, May, 1906   9.00
Merwin-Clayton, November, 1906   8.50
Anderson, October, 1907   7.10
Merwin-Clayton, January, 1908   5.00
Anderson, May, 1908   5.00

WEEK, 1868

Mackay sale, April, 1900 $7.00
Lockwood sale, October, 1902   5.00
May sale, January, 1903   3.00
French and Chubbuck sale, February, 1904   3.25
Anderson, December, 1904   3.50
Anderson, December, 1904   3.00
Anderson, June, 1905   3.00

WINTER, 1888, FIRST EDITION

Arnold sale, January, 1901 $5.00
Bangs, October, 1901   3.75
Brandon sale, February, 1906   4.50
Merwin-Clayton, May, 1906   7.75
O'Shaughnessy sale, April, 1907   4.60
Anderson, May, 1908   4.50

WRITINGS, LARGE-PAPER, 11 vols., 1894

Adee sale, November, 1895; uncut $35.75
Bangs, January, 1898; uncut   29.15
Libbie, January, 1899; uncut   26.12
Richmond sale, March 20; uncut   36.30
Peirce sale, March, 1903; uncut   60.50
Knapp sale, February, 1905; uncut   38.50

Pattee sale, December, 1905; uncut	$33.00
Fuller sale, February, 1907; uncut	51.15

WRITINGS, RIVERSIDE EDITION, 11 vols., 1894
Conely sale, October, 1902	$11.00

YANKEE IN CANADA, 1866, FIRST EDITION
Roos sale, April, 1897	$3.25
Mackay sale, April, 1900	3.50
Arnold sale, January, 1901	8.50
Anderson, February, 1901	3.25
Lockwood sale, October, 1902	5.62
Bangs, October, 1902	3.25
May sale, January, 1903	5.00
Anderson, May, 1903	6.00
Bartlett sale, May, 1903	5.00
Somerby sale, December, 1903	4.50
Anderson, January, 1904	4.00
French and Chubbuck sale, February, 1904	4.10
Stephens sale, April, 1904; stamps on title	3.00
Anderson, December, 1904	3.25
O'Shaughnessy sale, February, 1905	4.30
Drowne sale, December, 1905	5.50
Pyser sale, February, 1906	5.00
Searing sale, February, 1906	3.50
Peacock sale, March, 1906	3.50
Barry sale, May, 1906	4.25
Merwin-Clayton, May, 1906	3.00
Merwin-Clayton, January, 1908	3.00

MANUSCRIPTS

The descriptions of the several items in the following record are practically word for word as they appear in *American Book-Prices Current*.

LETTER of 1 page, 4to, Concord, October 9, 1841.
Bangs, April, 1896	$33.00

LETTER of 2 pages, 4to, 1856, to Mr. Blake.
Bangs, May, 1899	7.25

LETTER of 2 pages, 4to, Concord, February 16, 1849, to Geo. A. Thatcher. Personal letter.
Williamson sale, March, 1904 $46.00

LETTER of 3 pages, 8vo, Concord, July 11, 1857, addressed "Dear Cousin."
Williamson sale, March, 1904   35.00

AUTOGRAPH MANUSCRIPT of part of the essay on "Wild Apples," 8 pages, 4to.
Kennard sale, April, 1904   50.00

AUTOGRAPH MANUSCRIPT of part of the essay "Autumnal Tints," 6 pages, 4to.
Kennard sale, April, 1904   36.00

AUTOGRAPH MANUSCRIPT of part of "A Yankee in Canada," 5 pages, 4to.
Kennard sale, April, 1904   35.00

AUTOGRAPH MANUSCRIPT on "Conversation," 4 pages, 4to.
Knapp sale, February, 1905   31.00

LETTER of 1 page, 8vo, Concord, April 30, 1855, asking if it is not time to republish *A Week on the Concord and Merrimack Rivers.*
Alger sale, May, 1905   38.00

ORIGINAL AUTOGRAPH MANUSCRIPT OF "INDEPENDENCE," 2 pages, 4to, July 30, 1841.
Wilson sale, May, 1905   20.50

ORIGINAL AUTOGRAPH MANUSCRIPT of his nature diary for the years 1850 to 1861, inclusive, 90 pages, folio.
Wendell sale, May, 1905   145.00

ORIGINAL MANUSCRIPT NOTES on general phenomena of nature for the month of November, during the years 1850 to 1859, written on the backs of many business letters, 30 pages, 4to.
Wendell sale, May, 1905   75.00

ORIGINAL MANUSCRIPT NOTES of a natural history for the various months of the years 1851 to 1860, many pages written in ink and pencil on the backs of letters, 77 pages, 4to and 8vo.
Wendell sale, May, 1905 $50.00

ORIGINAL MANUSCRIPT, "The Flowering of Plants, accidentally observed in '51, with considerable care in '52; the spring of '51 being 10 days and more earlier than that of '52; the names those used by Gray," 38 pages, oblong folio.
Wendell sale, May, 1905   40.00

About twelve sheets of his ORIGINAL MANUSCRIPT of "Night and Moonlight."
Rutter sale, May, 1905   13.00

LETTER of 1 page, 8vo, Concord, September 1, 1856, to Lowell. "I shall be glad to receive payment for my story as soon as convenient — will you be so good as to direct it this way."
Moulton sale, November, 1905   27.50

ORIGINAL MANUSCRIPT NOTES on general phenomena of nature, 28 pages, 4to.
John Kendrick Bangs sale, November, 1905   33.00

AUTOGRAPH MANUSCRIPT POEM, entitled "Godfrey of Boulogne," 2 pages, 4to.
John Kendrick Bangs sale, November, 1905   35.00

MANUSCRIPT POEM, entitled "The Fog," written by him while at Harvard, 12 lines.
Anderson, December, 1905   16.00

ORIGINAL MANUSCRIPT NOTES on birds, insects, etc., 2 pages, 8vo.
Anderson, January, 1906   8.50

ORIGINAL MANUSCRIPT NOTES. Observations on the growth of the grasses, headed "Verdure," 2 pages, 8vo.
Anderson, January, 1906   8.00

ORIGINAL MANUSCRIPT NOTES. Observations on the wild quadrupeds about Concord, from 1850 to 1858, 4to.

Anderson, January, 1906 — $6.75

LETTER of 1 page, 4to, and envelope addressed [Feb. 11, 1859] to H. G. Denny, sending $5.00 to purchase books for Harvard College library.

Denny sale, January, 1906 — 36.00

LETTER of 1 page, small 4to, Concord, 1855, regarding changes in proof, perhaps for *Walden*.

Gebhard sale, February, 1906 — 22.00

RECEIPT for $400, signed, Concord, December 10, 1850.

Tefft sale, December, 1906 — 8.50

ORIGINAL AUTOGRAPH MANUSCRIPT, 3 pages, 4to. College exercise written during his sophomore year at Harvard [1835].

Anderson, May, 1907 — 45.00

AUTOGRAPH MANUSCRIPT of an essay on "The Love of Stories, real or fabulous, in young and old," 4 pages, 4to, 1836.

Merwin-Clayton, October, 1907 — 16.00

AUTOGRAPH MANUSCRIPT of one of his college papers, folded once and with his name in his own hand on the upper side of the outer leaf, 2 pages, 4to.

Anderson, November, 1907 — 15.25

LETTER of 1 page, 4to, Concord, October 30, 1854, to Charles Sumner.

Stickney sale, December, 1907 — 21.00

AUTOGRAPH MANUSCRIPT, headed "Show how it is that a writer's nationality and individual genius may be fully manifested in a play or other literary work upon a Foreign or Ancient subject," 9 pages, 4to.

Stickney sale, December, 1907 — 13.00

AUTOGRAPH MANUSCRIPT of 1 page of his " Maine
Woods," 4to.

Stickney sale, December, 1907 $9.50

SHORT LETTER in pencil, 1 page, oblong 12mo,
"Friday eve," to Mr. Sanborn.

Hess sale, January, 1908   5.30

NOTE, signed, at the bottom of a letter, 2 pages, of
Ralph Waldo Emerson, Concord, 23 July, 1850,
to Horace Greeley, franked by H. D. Thoreau.
In reference to the drowning of Margaret Fuller.

Sayre sale, April, 1908   35.00

APPENDIX

APPENDIX

A

A LIST OF THE POEMS AND BITS OF VERSE CONTAINED IN THOREAU'S PROSE WORKS EXCLUSIVE OF THE JOURNAL

A WEEK ON THE CONCORD AND MERRIMACK RIVERS

	First Edition	Second Edition	Riverside Edition	Walden Edition
"Where'er thou sail'st who sailed with me"	3	5	2	2
"I am bound, I am bound, for a distant shore"	4	6	2	2
"I sailed up a river with a pleasant wind"	5	7	2	2
"The respectable folks"	11	13	8	7
"Ah, 't is in vain the peaceful din"	20	23	18	15
"But since we sailed"	21	24	19	16
"Here then an aged shepherd dwelt"	21	24	19	16
"On Ponkawtasset, since we took our way"[1]	22	25	20	16
"Who sleeps by day and walks by night"	44	48	51	41
"An early unconverted Saint"	47	51	53	42
"Low in the eastern sky" (To the Maiden in the East)	51	54	58	46
"Dong, sounds the brass in the east"	54	58	62	50
"Greece, who am I that should remember thee"	59	62	68	54
"Some tumultuous little rill"	66	69	77	62
"I make ye an offer"	73	76	86	69
"Conscience is insti ct bred in the house" (Conscience)	79	82	94	75

[1] In the first edition this line reads, " On Ponkawtasset, since, with such delay."

	First Edition	Second Edition	Riverside Edition	Walden Edition
"Such waters do the gods distill"	88	92	107	86
"That Phaeton of our day"	105	107	128	103
"Then spend an age in whetting thy desire"	112	114	138	111
"Though all the fates should prove unkind"	151	155	189	151
"With frontier strength ye stand your ground" (Mountains)	168	173	212	170
"Here lies an honest man"	176	180	221	178
"The western wind came lumbering in"	178	182	224	180
"Then idle Time ran gadding by"	179	183	226	181
"Now chiefly is my natal hour"	180	184	226	182
Rumors from an Æolian Harp	181	185	229	184
"Away! away! away! away!"	183	187	231	186
"Ply the oars! away! away!" (River Song, part)	189	191	234	188
"Since that first 'Away! away!'" (River Song, part)	201	202	248	200
"Low-anchored cloud" (Mist)	201	203	249	201
"Man's little acts are grand"	223	225	279	224
"Our uninquiring corpses lie more low"	225	227	281	227
"The waves slowly beat"	227	229	284	229
"Woof of the sun, ethereal gauze" (Haze)	227	229	284	229
"Where gleaming fields of haze"	231	234	290	234
Translations from Anacreon	238	240	298	240
"Thus, perchance, the Indian hunter" (Boat Song)	245	247	306	247
"My life is like a stroll upon the beach" (The Fisher's Boy)	255	257	317	255
"This is my Carnac, whose unmeasured dome"	266	268	331	267
"True kindness is a pure divine affinity"	[1]	275	342	275
"Lately, alas, I knew a gentle boy" (Sympathy)	274	276	343	276
The Atlantides	276	278	345	278
"Love equals swift and slow"	285 [2]			

[1] These lines do not appear in the first edition.

[2] Only in the first edition. See p. 40.

	First Edition	Second Edition	Riverside Edition	Walden Edition
"My love must be as free" (Free Love)	293	296	369	297
"The Good how can we trust?"	294	298	371	298
"Nature doth have her dawn each day"	298	301	375	302
"Let such pure hate still underprop" (Friendship)	300	304	379	305
"Men are by birth equal in this, that given"	306	309	386	311
The Inward Morning	308	311	388	313
"My books I'd fain cast off, I cannot read" (The Summer Rain)	318	320	397	320
"My life has been the poem I would have writ"	362	364	453	365
The Poet's Delay	362	364	453	366
"I hearing get, who had but ears"	368	369	460	372
"Men dig and dive but cannot my wealth spend"	369	371	462	373
"Salmon Brook"	371	372	463	375
"Oft, as I turn me on my pillow o'er"	379	380	474	384
"I am the autumnal sun" (Nature's Child)	397	399	499	404
"A finer race and finer fed"	401	403	503	407
"I am a parcel of vain strivings tied" (Sic Vita)	403	405	506	410
"All things are current found"	408	410	512	415

WALDEN

	First Edition	Riverside Edition	Walden Edition
"Men say they know many things"	46	68	46
"What's the railroad to me?"	133	192	135
"It is no dream of mine"	209	303	215
"Light-winged Smoke, Icarian bird" (Smoke)	271	391	279

THE MAINE WOODS

"Die and be buried who will"	82	109	88

EXCURSIONS

"Within the circuit of this plodding life" (Winter Memories)	37	127	103

	First Edition	Riverside Edition	Walden Edition
"We pronounce thee happy, Cicada" (from Anacreon)	43	133	108
"His steady sail he never furls"	45	134	109
Return of Spring (from Anacreon)	45	135	109
"Each summer sound"	48	138	112
"Sometimes I hear the veery's clarion"	48	138	112
"Upon the lofty elm tree sprays" (The Vireo)	49	138	112
"Thou dusky spirit of the wood" (The Crow)	49	139	113
"I see the civil sun drying earth's tears" (The Thaw, part)	58	147	120
"The river swelleth more and more" (A River Scene)	58	148	120
"The needles of the pine"	73	163	133
"With frontier strength ye stand your ground" (Mountains)	73	163	133
"Not unconcerned Wachusett rears his head"	87	176	144
"The sluggish smoke curls up from some deep dell" (Smoke in Winter)	111	201	165
"When Winter fringes every bough" (Stanzas written at Walden)	125	215	176
The Old Marlborough Road	172	263	214
"In two years' time 't had thus"	282	372	303

B

ADDENDA

Note on

A WEEK ON THE CONCORD AND MERRIMACK RIVERS. New and Revised Edition. 1868.

This edition shows many emendations of a minor sort, probably taken from an annotated copy of the first edition left by Thoreau among his effects. Most of the alterations — additions, deletions, and substitutions — are clearly in the way of improvement, but one change it is not so easy to account for. The lines in "Saturday" which refer to Channing began in the first edition, —

> "On Ponkawtasset, since, with such delay,
> Down this still stream we took our meadowy way,
> A poet wise has settled, whose fine ray
> Doth faintly shine on Concord's twilight day."

In the second edition this stanza reads, —

> "On Ponkawtasset, since, we took our way,
> Down this still stream to far Billericay,
> A poet wise has settled, whose fine ray
> Doth often shine on Concord's twilight day."

The commas after "since" and "way" are clearly superfluous, and may be set down as due to a careless marking of the copy, which left the original punctuation of the line while it altered the words and the syntax. The difficulty is with the words, for the lines as thus altered seem no improvement over those of the first edition. They are, in fact, a partial return to a still earlier reading. Mr. Sanborn informs the writer that a set of proof-sheets of the first edition of the *Week*, with corrections by Thoreau, which has recently passed through his hands, shows that the lines as originally set up read as follows: —

> "On Ponkawtasset, since we took our way
> Down this fair stream toward neighboring Billerica,
> A poet wise has settled, whose fine ray
> Doth twinkle oft on Concord's twilight day."

This was corrected by the author to read as it appears in the first edition.

WALDEN. London: J. M. Dent & Co. New York: E. P. Dutton & Co. [1908.]

16mo, pp. xiv, 294. In Everyman's Library. Introduction by Walter Raymond.

CAPE COD. Illustrated by Clifton Johnson. New York: Thomas Y. Crowell & Co. [1908.]

8vo, pp. xii, 319. Photogravure frontispiece and 32 full-page half-tones. Introduction by Clifton Johnson.

BOOKS CONTAINING CRITICISM ON THOREAU

BORN, HELENA.

Whitman's Ideal Democracy, and Other Writings, pp. 20–30. Boston: Printed at the *Everett Press*. 1902.

An essay entitled "Thoreau's Joy in Nature."

FEDERN, KARL.

In Das Neunzehnte Jahrhundert in Bildnissen, herausgegeben von Karl Werckmeister, vol. iii, pp. 468, 469. Berlin: Kunstverlag der Photographischen Gesellschaft. 1899.

An account of Thoreau's life and work accompanying a half-tone portrait (No. 330 of the series) from one of the Maxham daguerreotypes.

JOHNSON, CLIFTON.

In Cape Cod, illustrated by Clifton Johnson, pp. v–viii. New York: Thomas Y. Crowell & Co. [1908.]

KENNEDY, WILLIAM SLOANE.

Poems of the Weird and Mystical, p. 9. Boston: Privately Printed. 1885.

A poem entitled " At Thoreau's Grave."

MORE, PAUL ELMER.

Shelburne Essays, Fifth Series, pp. 106–131. New York: G. P Putnam's Sons. 1908.

An essay entitled "Thoreau's Journal."

NEWSPAPER ARTICLE

1888

Concord Recollections. W. S. K. [William Sloane Kennedy].
  Boston Evening Transcript, September 15.
  Includes an account of a lecture on Thoreau given by Mr.
Kennedy in Concord in 1880, with reminiscential remarks
made by Messrs. Alcott and Sanborn after the lecture.

C

ERRATUM

Page 77. The second item under *Scribner's Monthly* belongs
of right to *Scribner's Magazine*, a publication which is of course
entirely separate from the former.

INDEX

INDEX

Titles of Thoreau's books are set in small capitals ; those of his poems articles, lectures, etc., in italics. Titles of books, articles, and poems by other writers are in roman within quotation-marks. Figures in italics indicate the page where a detailed description will be found, or where the first publication of an essay or piece of verse, or its appearance in Thoreau's Journal or manuscripts, is noted.